EGYPT

Compact Guide: Egypt is the ultimate quick-reference [guide to this destina]tion. It tells [you all you need to know ab]out the attractions of [the] country, from the [Pyramids of] Giza to the V[alley] of the Kings, the re[sor]ts [of the] Red Sea [to the] mountains of Sinai, a[nd fro]m the crowd[ed ba]zaars of Cairo to the rem[ote oa]ses of the d[esert].

This i[s one] of 1[3]3 Compact Gu[id]es p[rodu]ced by the e[ditors] of Insight Guides, w[hose] b[ook]s have set th[e stan]dard for visual tra[v]el g[uides] since 1970[. Pack]ed with inform[at]i[o]n, a[rrang]ed in easy-[to-follo]w routes, [an]d lavishly [illus]trated with p[hotogr]aphs, this book not only [guide]s you round[s it] but also gives you f[ascin]ating insigh[ts into] local life.

Insight Compact Guide: Egypt

Written by: Michel Rauch and David Ingram
Updated by: Chris Bradley
Photography by: Axel Krause and Sarah Louise Ramsay
Additional photography by: courtesy of Bloomsbury Publishing Plc 107;
Egyptian Tourist Board/Hemis.fr 75, 89; Pete Bennett 10/1, 13/1, 39, 55/1,
59/1, 63/1, 66/1, 72, 73/1, 78/1, 80, 98/1/2, 100, 106, 110; Chris Bradley/Apa
15, 33, 43/1, 96, 99, 115; Luc Chessex 22–3, 60/1, 61, 62, 64, 65/1/2, 79/1/2,
103/1; Glyn Genin/Apa 71, 76; Topham Picturepoint 19, 109
Cover picture by: 4Corners Images
Picture Editor: Hilary Genin
Maps: Maria Randell

Series Editor: Carine Tracanelli
Edited by: Tom Stainer

CONTACTING THE EDITORS: As every effort is made to provide accurate information in this publication, we would appreciate it if readers would call our attention to any errors and omissions by contacting:
Apa Publications, PO Box 7910, London SE1 1WE, England.
Fax: (44 20) 7403 0290
e-mail: insight@apaguide.co.uk

Information has been obtained from sources believed to be reliable, but its accuracy and completeness, and the opinions based thereon, are not guaranteed.

© 2010 APA Publications GmbH & Co. Verlag KG Singapore Branch, Singapore.

First Edition 1995; Second Edition 2003; Third Edition 2010
Printed in Singapore by Insight Print Services (Pte) Ltd
Original edition © Polyglott-Verlag Dr Bolte KG, Munich

Worldwide distribution enquiries:
Apa Publications GmbH & Co. Verlag KG (Singapore Branch)
38 Joo Koon Road, Singapore 628990
Tel: (65) 6865-1600, apasin@signet.com.sg

Distributed in the UK & Ireland by:
GeoCenter International Ltd
Meridian House, Churchill Way West
Basingstoke, Hampshire RG21 6YR
sales@geocenter.co.uk

Distributed in the United States by:
Langenscheidt Publishers, Inc.
36–36 33rd Street 4th Floor, Long Island City, NY 11106
orders@langenscheidt.com

www.insightguides.com

Introduction

Places

Culture

Practical Information

◁ **Valley of the Kings (p59)** The Tomb of Tutankhamun is the most famous of these pharaohs' graves, built to preserve their mummified bodies for eternity.

▽ **Red Sea Coast (p87)** Beautiful sandy beaches, turquoise seas, coral reefs and exotic fish attract tourists all year round.

△ **Aswan (p74)** A *felucca* (sailboat) ride is the ideal way to enjoy the charm of Aswan.

▷ **St Catherine's (p96)** The monastery has a wonderful icon collection.

◁ **Cairo (p24)** A moment of calm in the multicultural melting pot of Egypt's capital.

▷ **Alexandria (p45)** This cosmopolitan city was once dubbed the 'pearl of the Mediterranean'.

△ **Siwah Oasis (p90)**
In the middle of the Libyan Desert stands this isolated oasis, where an independent culture has flourished along with the best dates in Egypt.

△ **Giza (p38)**
The Pyramids of Giza, the only survivors among the Seven Wonders of the Ancient World, rise dramatically from a plateau on the edge of the Western Desert.

◁ **Abu Simbel (p78)**
These huge temples and colossal statues were intended to show the might of Egypt and deter would-be invaders.

▷ **Luxor and Karnak (p55)** The Temple of Luxor was connected to Karnak's great Temple of Amun by an Avenue of Sphinxes. Both temples show the desire of successive pharaohs to outdo their predecessor.

An Ancient Land

Egypt's pharaonic heritage is both a curse and a blessing. A blessing because tourism is one of the state's most important sources of income, with more than 9 million visitors a year. A curse because, in the minds of most visitors, the vast and magnificent relics of Egypt's past eclipse all other aspects of the country. Few visitors want to see beyond the Pyramids, the Valley of the Kings, the famous temples and historic mosques. Unless, of course, they are divers or sun worshippers. In which case, the Red Sea Coast and Sinai Peninsula will be favoured destinations. However, the culture of modern Egypt can be just as interesting as its ancient history and its diving, and travellers can enrich their experience of the country if they look beyond the classic destinations and received preconceptions.

This predominantly Islamic country has been open to mass tourism for many years. It offers a well-developed infrastructure and the locals are used to having foreigners in their midst. The images of the country that appear in the Western media are often distorted by headlines. Fundamentalism does not just mean violent terrorism and a political movement shrouded in a religious mantle that is shaking the nation's foundations. It also means a return to religious values, to social obligations and to traditions that are not dictated by outside cultures.

Egypt is an extremely friendly country and guests are heartily welcomed. They are asked a whole series of curious questions about their family, their work, and what they think of Egypt. Often they will be offered a glass of tea and welcomed into family homes.

The classic tour of the Pyramids, Thebes and Luxor is certainly recommended for first-time visitors to Egypt, but the country has much more to offer. Between Al-Arish and Marsa Matruh on the Mediterranean – 'the Egyptian Riviera' where the Egyptians themselves go for their holidays – the sea is a brilliant turquoise-blue, with palm-lined beaches and a few remaining deserted

The weight of history
Egypt's recorded history is one of the longest known to archaeologists. The earliest hieroglyphic texts to have been found date from around 3,150 BC. By this time the writing system was fully formed so it is conjectured that earlier forms of writing are yet to be found. It is because of the vast, and varied, amount of information recorded by ancient scribes that we know so much about ancient Egyptian society, religion and culture.

Opposite: a felucca on the Nile near Aswan
Below: a relief from the temple of Kom Ombo

The Nile

Egypt only exists because of the River Nile, which starts off in two African lakes 1,600km (1,000 miles) apart, as the Blue and White Nile. By some whim of nature the rivers did not flow the obvious way into the Indian Ocean, but chose the long and hard journey to the Mediterranean, through some of the most arid regions in Africa. The Nile did not just make it through the desert, but at the hottest time of the year the river managed to flood the riverbanks and cover the fields with rich alluvial soil. As a result, the Delta has some of the most fertile land in the world.

bays. The Libyan Desert, where time seems to stand still, is a paradise in its own right. Desert covers 96 percent of the country, and it provides an unforgettable natural spectacle, with dunes, rocks, fossils and myriad colours ranging from ochre to dark red (the nomads have names for all of them). Trips across this desert – which was referred to in antiquity as the 'Ocean of Fire' – are wonderfully sensual experiences as well as great physical challenges.

Many of Egypt's visitors down the centuries have returned again and again. The most famous of them recorded their experiences for posterity: from the ancient Greeks – the historian Herodotus, for instance, the geographer Strabo and the mathematician Euclid – to authors closer to our time – Gustave Flaubert, Agatha Christie, Lawrence Durrell and EM Forster.

This land was equally fascinating for the men who conquered it: Alexander the Great, who gave it the city of Alexandria, the 'Pearl of the Mediterranean'; and Napoleon, whose scholars and archaeologists rediscovered Ancient Egypt. The French emperor made a stirring address to his troops at the Pyramids: 'Men, forty centuries are looking down at you!'

And should visiting all the monuments and mosques tire you out, you can rest assured that you are in illustrious company. The French novelist Gustave Flaubert confessed so much in his *Egyptian Diary*: 'I find Egyptian temples indescribably tedious...'

POSITION AND SIZE

Egypt is located in the northeastern corner of Africa; the capital is Cairo. The Arab Republic of Egypt, or *Gumhuria Al-Arabia Al-Masria*, measures about 1,055km (655 miles) from north to south, and around 1,050km (652 miles) from east to west at its widest point, and is bordered to the east by Israel, the Gulf of Aqaba, and the Red Sea; to the south by the Sudan; to the west by Libya; and to the north by the Mediterranean.

Egypt occupies a total surface area of 1,001,450sq km (387,000sq miles), and 96 percent of the country is arid desert. The remaining 4 percent lies along the life-giving River Nile, which has a total length of 6,671km (4,145 miles), flowing north across a narrow ribbon of fertile land in places no more than a mile (1.6km) wide.

Geographically, Egypt comprises five different landscapes: the Nile Valley, the Nile Delta, the Libyan Desert, the Sinai and the Eastern or Arabian Desert, which was a green tropical forest only 15,000 years ago.

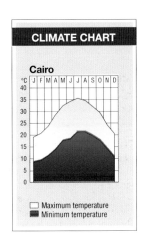

CLIMATE CHART

Cairo

□ Maximum temperature
■ Minimum temperature

CLIMATE – WHEN TO GO

There are major differences in climate between the south and north of the country, and this may influence the choice of when to go.

For Upper Egypt (the southern part near the 'upper reaches' of the Nile), October until early May is the best time, especially for those who don't like the heat, and for Cairo, September until early May, but bear in mind that the weather here in winter (December to March) is cool, cloudy and often rainy.

The Mediterranean coast has high summer temperatures from May until September but the winters tend to be cold and rainy, with even the odd brief snowfall. The Red Sea and the Sinai

A dramatic view from Mount Moses in the Sinai

have summer temperatures all year round, and the climate is extremely dry and hot between May and September.

The bathing temperature of the Red Sea seldom drops below 20°C (68°F); in the Mediterranean, temperatures exceed 20°C (68°F) only between May and September.

Between March and May the '50-day-long' desert wind known as the *Khamsin* (the Arabic word for 50) can blow dry and hot air as well as a lot of sand and dust from the desert.

Below: bullrushes by the Nile
Bottom: wind-sculpted rock in the White Desert

NATURE AND ENVIRONMENT

Arable land in Egypt is entirely confined to the Nile valley and delta, and the crops include corn (maize), rice, wheat, millet, pumpkins, dates, sugar cane, tomatoes, herbs, spices, cotton, watermelons, oranges, onions and potatoes. The Nile river is lined with date palms, and fruit and vines grow abundantly in the oases and in the delta. The river and irrigation canals support many varieties of water plants, although the papyrus of antiquity is now found only in botanical gardens. The Mediterranean coast has palm-lined beaches, while the Sinai peninsula has wild and rocky mountain landscapes with deep gorges. The oases are like small paradises in the middle of the desert, with groves, plantations and fields of grain.

Despite the lack of pastureland, livestock is kept on farms and includes goats, sheep and poultry. Cattle, water buffalo, horses, donkeys and camels are used as working animals and also for transport. The many species of bird include birds of prey (such as kites), herons and hoopoes. Ironically, the falcon, a symbol of power throughout Arab countries and a popular emblem (it appears on Egypt's flag), is threatened with extinction. Egypt suffers from a chronic lack of water, as the Nile is increasingly saline because of its much reduced flow due to the Aswan Dam and over-irrigation.

Interest in ecology is a luxury in a land as impoverished as Egypt. Cairo is battling with one of the highest levels of air pollution in the world, and many inhabitants suffer from chronic respiratory diseases as a result of permanent smog. Protecting national parks, mainly in the southern Sinai and outside Hurghada, has created its own problems: mass tourism means more waste and greater water consumption, while marine life is threatened by divers and the careless use of anchors on coral reefs. Oil tankers passing through the Suez Canal are a threat to life in the Red Sea. Things are changing very slowly as awareness of these problems is growing, and more is being done to combat pollution.

POPULATION

At present Egypt has a population of over 81 million, and the number is increasing by 1.3 million annually. Greater Cairo now contains more than 20 million people, a figure that represented the entire population of the country in the 1950s.

The dominant physical characteristics of Egypt's population are the result of the admixture of Hamitic and Semitic peoples. Minority groups in the country include the Nubians (in the southern part of the Nile Valley), the Hamitic Beja (in the southern section of the Eastern Desert), Beduins (in Sinai and along the Red Sea Coast) and peoples of mixed Arab and Berber stock (in the Western Desert).

Population explosion
The key social question in Egypt is the high birth rate, which makes great demands on the country's resources, economy and social services. The government set up the National Population Council in 1985, which made birth control readily available. Since then, the birth rate has dropped from 39 to fewer than 24 per 1,000 people, but Egypt's population is still growing fast and is predicted to reach 123 million by 2025. The growing influence of Islamic fundamentalists, who are opposed to contraception, could see the rate accelerate once more. The population explosion is only just being kept under control. Children are the only guarantee of security in old age and campaigns to curb population growth have had little success: a baby is born here every 24 seconds.

A man pressing linen in a Cairo laundry

👁 **Religious tension**
Since the 1980s Islamic fundamentalists have been trying to overthrow the government and replace it with a pure Islamic state. The main targets have been the security forces and government officials, and in the 1990s their campaign turned into terrorist attacks against tourists, but all along they have also attacked the many churches and Christians, especially in Upper Egyptian villages. The government does all it can to protect tourism, and security is very tight throughout the country. Tourists can therefore travel between cities in Upper Egypt only in armed convoy.

Most of Egypt's workforce is employed in the service industries (46 percent of the working population) and agriculture (33 percent). The *fellahin*, Egypt's peasants, form the conservative core of the Nile Valley's inhabitants. Economic hardship forces many of them to seek work in Cairo or Alexandria, but with such a high illiteracy rate – just over 50 percent of Egyptians (mainly women) cannot read or write – their chances of success are not high.

Egypt no longer has anything like the resources to feed its growing population, and today more than half of the country's food needs to be imported, paid for with valuable foreign currency.

RELIGION IN MODERN EGYPT

The official religion of Egypt is Islam, and about 90 percent of the population is Muslim, nearly all of them Sunnites. Most of the Christian minority are Copts, who, despite their constitutional rights, are politically under-represented. Butros Butros-Ghali is a Copt who has achieved prominence in public life. He was deputy prime minister of Egypt before serving as General Secretary of the UN from 1992–96.

Terrorist fundamentalists have been trying to fan the flames of dissent between Muslims and Copts, but without any marked success. The once-powerful Jewish community has dwindled substantially since the creation of Israel in 1948 and the consecutive wars with Israel – Egypt's few remaining synagogues are deserted these days.

ISLAM

Islam is the most recent of the three great monotheistic world religions. It was founded by Abul Kasim Muhammad Ibn Abd Allah, a merchant who was born around AD570 in Mecca (now in Saudi Arabia). Known as Muhammad, this merchant was chosen as the Prophet of God (Allah), and from AD609 he began to receive divine messages through the archangel Gabriel. Muhammad himself was illiterate, but his

Much work on the land is still done by hand

disciples later transcribed these messages into the Koran (Qur'an), the holy scripture of Islam, with 114 chapters of revelations. The Koran is regarded by Muslims as the ultimate authority, complemented by the Sunnah, which lists the sayings and actions of Prophet Muhammad, a section of which is known as the Hadith. As he became more popular and powerful, Prophet Muhammad was forced to flee from Mecca to Medina in AD622. This event, known as *al-Higra*, marks the start of the Islamic calendar still used today.

The Qur'an sees Jews and Christians as 'people of the Book', who received the message of the one true God, but who could not stay true to it. Muslims recognize Abraham, Moses and Jesus as prophets who revealed the true religion, but Prophet Muhammad is the last of the prophets.

Islamic thought differs from Christian thought on central issues. It denies the existence of original sin, for instance, and also Jesus's death on the Cross. It also denies that Jesus was the Son of God because God cannot beget nor be begotten.

When it comes to defining the word 'Islam', the notion of 'submission to the will of Allah' is a mere approximation. The Muslim faith is based on the Five Pillars of Islam: to recite publicly the profession of faith ('There is no God but Allah, and Muhammad is his Prophet'); to observe the five daily prayers at specific times in the direction

Below: Friday prayers in Cairo
Bottom: Alexandria's Abu al-Abbas mosque

*Below: a village on
Elephantine Island, Aswan
Bottom: a Haji's house,
Luxor West Bank*

of Mecca; to pay the *zakat* (purification) tax for the support of the poor or for the defence of Islam; to fast from daybreak to sunset during the holy month of Ramadan; and to perform the *haj* pilgrimage to the city of Mecca in Saudi Arabia at least once in a lifetime, if one has the means. Laymen often add a sixth pillar, that of *jihad*, which can be loosely translated as 'holy militancy', based on the notion of being or becoming a better and more God-fearing person. Missions to convert heathens do not form part of the basic tenets of Islam.

Muhammad died without naming a successor, and after his death the Muslims were divided. The Prophet's companion Abu Bakr became the first Caliph (successor of Muhammad as ruler of the Islamic world), but Ali, his son-in-law, claimed that he was the natural leader. The Sunnites, who include the majority of Egyptians, refused any of the Prophet's descendants as caliph, while the Shiite sect believe the descendants of Ali and Muhammad to be the true leaders.

Islam has a strong influence on the family and society. The most fundamental religious concept of Islam in Egypt is the *Shariah*, or the Law, although not all its tenets are followed to the letter: Egypt does without such draconian punishments as chopping off the hands of thieves, for instance, and is attempting to achieve some kind of harmonious balance between Islamic and modern laws.

The conqueror Amr Ibn al-As introduced Islam to Egypt in AD642, but the population managed to hold on to the Christian faith for a long time afterwards. Forcible Islamisation only took place several centuries later under Fatimid and Mamluk rule. Many Christians and other non-Muslims ended up embracing Islam 'voluntarily' – to avoid paying protection money.

THE COPTIC CHRISTIANS

The Arabic word *cupt*, westernised as Copt, is derived from the Greek word *Aigyptos* (Egyptian). The Copts regard themselves as the direct descendants of the ancient Egyptians and the early Christians. A theological conflict arose between the Copts and the Greek-speaking Romans, or Melchites, over the Council of Chalcedon in AD451; this rejected their Monophysite doctrine (belief in the single nature and therefore physical divinity of Christ).

The Coptic Church is led by a patriarch (at present Pope Shenouda III), who resides in Cairo. Egyptian Copts are every bit as fervent as their Muslim compatriots, and the increasing number of churchgoers is just one sign of the recent religious revival – possibly a reaction to the Islamic renaissance of the past few years. Copts pray and fast conscientiously (they eat no meat or dairy products), and their liturgy, which uses the ancient Coptic language, is based on the Eastern Orthodox tradition.

Monasticism in Egypt
In the 3rd and 4th centuries many Christians sought refuge in the desert from persecution by the Romans. St Anthony and St Paul became hermits in a cave in the Red Sea Mountains, and their followers gathered in settlements at the foot of the mountain. St Pachom, who served in the Roman army, went a step further and founded around 320AD the first monastic community. Influenced by his military life, he was convinced that monks should adhere to strict rules. His principles formed the basis of monasticism throughout the Christian church.

LANGUAGE

Everyday spoken Egyptian is an Arabic vernacular, while official Egyptian uses literary Arabic, whose form has remained substantially unchanged since it was introduced to the country with the Arab conquests almost 13 centuries ago. Arabic script runs from right to left, but beware: numbers go from left to right. Anyone eager to decipher coins and numbers would do

A service in progress in Cairo's Hanging Church

International relations
Following the 1979 peace treaty with Israel, Egypt developed closer relations with the United States. Egypt is now the second-largest recipient of international aid, after Israel. Its important political and military support for the US-led Gulf War in 1990 was rewarded with massive economic aid from Saudi Arabia. Relations with Iran, which supports Islamic groups in Egypt, are tense. President Mubarak strongly believes that Egypt should play a key role in the peace process in the Middle East, as the regional stability will help the country to overcome its domestic problems. Like most other Arab countries, Egypt was opposed to the recent US-led wars in Iraq and Afghanistan.

well to study Arabic numerals (not to be confused with our own 'Romanised' Arabic numerals). English is often readily understood in Cairo and Alexandria, and in tourist areas. Road signs are usually in Arabic with their transliterated equivalents; people heading off the beaten track should certainly arm themselves with a phrase book.

CUSTOMS AND RITUALS

The rhythm of daily life in Egypt is determined by the Islamic faith. Five times a day believers are called noisily to prayer through loudspeakers by the *muezzin*, and night becomes day in the month of Ramadan, when fasting during the day gives way to feasting after sunset.

That's when public life slows down almost to a halt; government offices work from 10 in the morning until two in the afternoon or, as an old Egyptian joke about efficiency goes, 'from 10 until a quarter to 10'.

Islamisation put a stop to many pharaonic customs, yet some have survived, mainly in rural areas. Belly-dancing continues, although now under severe pressure from radicals. The desire for children means that fertility cults thrive, often practised in secret at the ruins of ancient pharaonic sites. Each cult's activities are given superficial justification by the presence of a neighbouring holy tomb.

The traditional robe, now worn mainly by the rural population, is the *galabiyyah*, a long shirt-like garment, in white or light-blue. In public, women in rural areas cover their otherwise bright, shimmering robes with a black cloak. In deference to the return to Islamic values (and sometimes as a result of pressure from husbands or families), many women particularly in the cities are donning the *higab*, or veil (it covers the hair, but not the whole face).

The Hammam al-Sultan in Cairo

THE ECONOMY

Egypt is a developing country with an annual per capita income to match (around US$5,400).

Some 28 percent of the Egyptian workforce is employed in agriculture, which has an overwhelmingly commercial rather than subsistance basis, unlike in other comparable developing countries. This has been made possible by an almost unparalleled intensification of cultivation. In the 19th century, the ancient system of canals along the Nile Valley was repaired and extended. Barrages were also built, making feasible the production of summer cash crops. Nowadays, the export of cash crops, including cotton, potatoes and citrus fruits, remains a vital source of foreign exchange. But developments along the Nile have also brought problems. Completed in 1971, the Aswan High Dam may have put a stop to water shortages and perennial flooding, but it has also resulted in the loss of much fertile land, through waterlogging and salinity caused by constant use of irrigation water with not enough drainage. Massive amounts of fertiliser also have to be used to replace the natural silt of the Nile which no longer reaches many areas.

Below: bread making and (bottom) woodworkers

Textile and food factories are the backbone of the country's industry. Domestic deposits provide the raw material for the huge iron-and-steel combine in Helwan. Durable consumer goods such as refrigerators, television sets and cars are being produced as a result of several joint ventures with manufacturers from the US and Europe.

Electricity is mainly provided by renewable sources of energy, including the hydroelectric power stations at Aswan. Solar energy – most appropriate for Egypt's climate – is no longer in its infancy, and in February 1994 Egypt's first wind farm, one of the largest in Africa, was opened near Hurghada on the Red Sea, with an annual capacity of 15 million kilowatts of electricity. The country also has ample natural oil and gas deposits.

Egypt has four main sources of income that can fluctuate in response to external factors: tourism; Suez Canal tolls; money transfers from Egyptians living abroad; and crude oil exports. Imports overshadow profits from exports, with annual trade deficits averaging US$7.3 billion. Economic progress is hampered by the massive foreign debt, which is now around US$30 billion. The revision of decades-old laws and privatisation of state-owned industries – a legacy of the era of Arabic socialism – is a continuous process. Egypt now has an annual growth rate of about 7.2 percent.

POLITICS AND THE STATE

The head of state of the Arab Republic of Egypt and the commander-in-chief of its armed forces is the president, the *Rais*. The strong influence of the head of the executive on presidential democracy

Below: heavy industry near Cairo
Bottom: Alexandria's Corniche

became evident in the autumn of 1993, when the law stating that a president may be re-elected only once was altered specially for the incumbent Hosni Mubarak. In 2005 Mubarak was elected to his fifth six-year term of office. Under Mubarak, the ruling National Democratic Party calls all the shots. Early in 2005, Mubarak announced a change in the constitution to allow for multi-candidate presidential elections to be held that same year. These did go ahead but the National Democratic Party retained its huge majority and Mubarak is still in power. The opposition Muslim Brotherhood did make a breakthrough, however, taking around 20 percent of the votes. With 210 members, the Shura Council is an advisory body only.

In the country with probably the oldest bureaucracy in the world, administration is centred on Cairo. The constitution of 1971, which elevated Islam to a state religion, also granted more responsibilities to provincial governors and mayors.

Ever since the murder of President Sadat in 1981, emergency legislation has made life easier for those at the top and also given the police far more powers of arrest. Democratisation of the country, which had seemed so promising when Mubarak came to power, is proceeding at a snail's pace. Predictably, Western diplomats in Cairo collude in this by saying that the introduction of Western-style democracy might cause the country to collapse. 'Egypt,' according to one diplomat, 'is a pressure cooker – the lid is only being kept on because of counter-pressure.' This counter-pressure is provided in part by the army, which no president seems able to control. Every Egyptian head of state since the king's fall from power in 1952 has come from its ranks.

Terrorist attacks by fundamentalists on politicians, policemen, tourists and banks have resulted in a strong backlash by the security forces, and Egypt's record of human rights abuse continues to attract international condemnation. The future direction of the country is uncertain. President Hosni Mubarak turned 81 in 2009 and is yet to indicate whether he will run for head of state in the 2011 election.

Friendly warning
President Mubarak says that he warned the US of a possible terrorist attack 12 days before the World Trade Center was struck on September 11 2001. "We expected that something was going to happen and informed the Americans," he said. "But nobody expected the event would be of such enormity."

Hosni Mubarak in full flow

HISTORICAL HIGHLIGHTS

Until 3050BC Predynastic Period. *Homo erectus* lives as a nomadic hunter and gatherer in Egypt; nomads form first settlements along the Nile.

3050–2715BC Early Dynastic or Archaic Period (1st and 2nd dynasties). Upper and Lower Egypt united, traditionally by the first pharaoh, Menes (identical with King Hor Aha). New capital founded at Memphis. Hieroglyphics appear for the first time.

2715–2192BC Old Kingdom (3rd–6th dynasties). King Zoser's chief of works, Imhotep, begins pyramid construction with the step pyramid at Saqqarah. Pyramids built as monuments to the power of pharaohs of the 4th Dynasty (Sneferu, Cheops, Chephren, Mycerinus). Decentralisation of power into the hands of nobles, leading to collapse of central administration.

2192–2040BC First Intermediate Period (7th–10th dynasties). Lack of central authority, bad harvests. Civil wars usher in a phase of social and cultural change.

2040–1650BC Middle Kingdom (11th–14th dynasties). Mentuhotep II unites Upper and Lower Egypt, Thebes becomes a political and cultural centre, and Amun becomes the imperial deity. Provincial nobles deprived of power, Nubia conquered.

1650–1540BC Second Intermediate Period (15th–17th dynasties). Egypt conquered by the Hyksos from the Near East. Introduction of new military techniques such as use of cavalry and chariots. Medical treatise on wounds and surgery recorded on papyrus.

1540–1070BC New Kingdom (18th–20th dynasties). Age of the great pharaohs such as Amenhotep I–III, Tuthmosis I–IV, Queen Hatshepsut, Akhenaten, Ramesses I–IX and Tutankhamun. Domestic peace and prosperity. Egypt becomes a great power. Akhenaten replaces all gods with the Aten as the new state deity; Tutankhamun later reintroduces the cult of Amun and the old gods.

1070–332BC Late Dynastic Period (21st–30th dynasties). Foreign rule: Libyans and Ethiopians run Egypt. In 526BC Psamtik II, the last pharaoh of the 26th dynasty, is defeated by the Persians and Egypt becomes a Persian satrapy.

332–30BC The Ptolemies. Alexander the Great conquers Egypt and founds Alexandria. After his death, the dynasty of the Ptolemies takes over, founded by Alexander's general Ptolemy. Cleopatra (51–30BC) extends her dominion under the auspices of Caesar and Antony.

30BC–AD640 Roman Period. Egypt, a Roman province since the time of Octavian (Augustus), is exploited by Rome as an imperial granary. Christianity begins to spread; monks and hermits appear. Soon the Christians are persecuted. After the Council of Chalcedon in 451 the Egyptian (Coptic) Church splits from the imperial one.

From AD642 Islamisation of Egypt. In 642 the Arab general Amr Ibn al-As conquers Egypt and founds Fustat. Egypt is now ruled and plundered in turn by the Ummayyads, Abbasids, Tulunids, Ikhshids, Fatimids, Ayyubids and, from 1250, the Mamluks, slave soldiers of Turkish origin and their descendants.

1517–1798 Egypt is an Ottoman province. Sultan Salim I subjugates the country, and it loses its economic and cultural importance.

1798–9 Napoleon invades Egypt on the pretext of securing the authority of the Ottoman sultan, but in reality to control the land route and thwart British interests. His army defeats the Mamluks at the Pyramids. Britain's Admiral Nelson sinks Napoleon's fleet near Abu Qir.

1805–49 The Albanian Muhammad Ali becomes pasha and Turkish governor of Egypt. He drives the English out of the country and has his Mamluk rivals put to death. His reforms of the country's economy, army and education system lay the foundations of modern Egypt.

1869–1914 In 1869 the costly Suez Canal is opened, and in 1875 the British acquire the majority of shares in it. Nationalist uprisings are quashed in 1882 by the British occupation of Egypt; a rigid colonial regime fans the flames of independence and leads to the formation of the Nationalist Party.

1914–53 Egypt becomes a British protectorate in 1914 and an independent parliamentary monarchy in 1922 under King Fuad I. British military and political influence continues to fuel the independence movement led by Saad Zaghlul. In 1937 Farouk I ascends the throne. Egypt remains neutral during World War II, but is reoccupied by Britain. In 1946 the British limit their occupation of the country to the area surrounding the Suez Canal. In 1948 Egypt loses out to Israel in the Arab struggle against the new Jewish state.

1952–3 General Naguib's dissident officers (including Nasser and Sadat) depose Egypt's unpopular King Farouk in 1952 (Fires of Black Saturday), and on 18 June 1953 they declare the country a republic. All royal properties are nationalised.

1956 After the British withdrawal, President Nasser's nationalisation of the Suez Canal Company sparks off the Suez Crisis. Israel occupies the Sinai, and England and France send in troops. The UN negotiates a cease-fire and the withdrawal of all troops.

1967 Israel takes the Sinai Peninsula during the Six-Day War.

1970 Nasser dies and is succeeded by Anwar al-Sadat, who seeks reconciliation with the West. Aswan Dam opened by Sadat the following year.

1973 Egypt invades Sinai.

1974–9 Open Door Policy brings political liberalisation. The removal of subsidies on food in 1977 leads to riots.

1979 Sadat and the Israeli prime minister, Menachem Begin, sign the Camp David Agreement. Egypt is then banished from the Arab League.

1981 Islamic militants assassinate President Sadat. He is succeeded by Mohammed Hosni Mubarak.

1989 Israel returns the Sinai. Egypt is welcomed back into the Arab League.

From 1992 Muslim fundamentalists attack shops, tourists, Nile steamers, journalists, bankers and politicians.

1997 Work begins on the Toshka Canal, planned to irrigate the Libyan Desert.

2005 Multi-candidate presidential elections are held for the first time. President Mubarak's term is extended to 2011. A bomb explodes in Dahab, killing 20.

2008 Riots break out over the soaring cost of basic foods.

2009 US President Barack Obama visits Cairo and delivers a historic speech to the Muslim world.

Map on page 25

Cairo metropolis

'He who has not seen Cairo cannot know the grandeur of Islam. It is the metropolis of the universe, the garden of the world, the nest of human species, the gateway to Islam, the throne of royalty: it is a city embellished with castles and palaces and adorned with monasteries and dervishes, and with colleges lit by the moons and stars of erudition.' – Ibn Khaldun, 14th-century Arab historian.

Preceeding pages: Sultan Hassan and Ar-Rifai Mosques, Cairo
Below: traffic and cinema poster in modern Cairo

1: Cairo

Cairo, the largest city in Africa, is a multicultural melting pot, a modern-day metropolis and a magnificent Oriental bazaar all rolled into one. Its reputation for dust, filth, noise and chaos, though valid, is only part of the picture in this city of 18 million people (about a quarter of the country's population). Visitors eager to encounter the real Cairo, and not just the city of pyramids and mosques, should head for the narrow alleys in the old part of the city, where Cairenes treat the streets as their living room, and in some cases live in cemeteries. The people here are no less friendly or hospitable than anywhere else in Cairo, and a genuine interest is taken in foreigners – not just in the *baksheesh* they might provide.

HISTORY

The first capital of Egypt was Memphis, founded in c3100BC and now a suburb on the left bank of the river, 37km (23 miles) south of the city centre. When the Muslims arrived in Egypt under general Amr Ibn al-As, they founded Fustat ('the encampment'). Like Muhammad, al-As came from Mecca, but until his conversion he had been one of the strongest critics of Islam. It was only in AD969, after Egypt had been conquered by the Shiite Fatimids, that the foundation stone of today's Cairo was laid to the north of a group of towns that formed Greater Fustat. This city was called Al-Qahira ('the Invincible') and nicknamed Umm ed-Dunya ('Mother of the World').

From 1250 to 1517 Egypt was ruled by the Mamluks, who were descendants of Turkish, Caucasian and African slaves. Though brutal and barbarous, they were also responsible for providing the city with a great number of mosques, palaces, mausoleums and Koranic schools. Some say that the Mamluks built more than 20,000 palaces, but relatively few of them have survived. Cairo's heyday ended as the Middle Ages drew to a close, and by the beginning of the 16th century it had become nothing more than a sleepy provincial town. It was only in 1805 that it was jerked out of its slumber by the reform policies of Muhammad Ali, the father of modern Egypt.

SIGHTS

Five tours of the city are described here. Visitors planning to make only a short stopover in Cairo should at least visit the Egyptian Museum, some mosques (Al-Azhar, Ibn Tulun Mosque, Mosque of Sultan Hassan), the Khan al-Khalili Bazaar and the Pyramids.

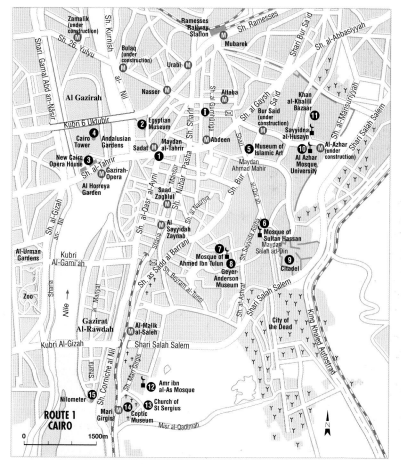

Map
on page
25

*Below: Ramesses II
Bottom: Maydan
al-Tahrir at night*

TOUR 1

Maydan al-Tahrir ❶ with the Sadat metro station is the most important square in the city. Standing around it, starting clockwise from the eastern end, are the former American University, the Ministry of the Interior, the Mugamma (the semi-circular concrete complex), the Arab League building and the Nile Hilton.

A GREAT MUSEUM

The most interesting building in the square, however, and one of the highlights of any trip to Egypt, is the ★★★**Egyptian Museum ❷** (open daily 9am–6pm; 9am–3pm in Ramadan; no cameras), next to the Hilton. Its unique collection of antiquities was started by the French Egyptologist Auguste Mariette, and its 155,000 exhibits document 4,500 years of Egyptian history.

The collection has long outgrown the space provided, and a larger building is planned near the Pyramids of Giza. The museum is vast, and for the visitor with limited time it is recommended to concentrate on specific exhibits.

GROUND FLOOR

Right next to the entrance is the massive 10-metre (33-ft) statue of Amenhotep III from the New

Kingdom and his wife, Queen Tiye, a Syrian princess famed for her beauty.

Finds from the Old Kingdom (2715–2192BC**)**

Gallery 42: The 5th Dynasty wooden statue of Ka'aper, a high priest of Memphis, was jokingly referred to as the 'village mayor' by the workmen who dug it up in 1861, because it reminded them of their local mayor. There is a superb statue of Chephren in black diorite, from his valley temple in Giza.

Gallery 32: Expressions of love can be seen with the family portraits of Rahotep and Nofret, and the dwarf Seneb and his family.

Finds from the Middle Kingdom (2040–1650BC**)**

Gallery 22: The cedarwood figurine of King Sesostris I that was found near the royal pyramid of Al-Lisht is just 60cm (2ft) high. This statue, which shows the pharaoh with the crown of Upper Egypt, had a counterpart which has been lost; all that remains of it is the crown of Lower Egypt, which is on display in the Metropolitan Museum, New York.

Finds from the New Kingdom (1550–1070BC**)**

Gallery 3 (Amarnah Gallery): The pieces from the Akhenaton era are particularly striking because their artistic style breaks completely with tradition. Displayed here are colossal statues of the ruler, Akhenaton, and paintings from his palaces. Popular exhibits carved from reddish quartzite are the unfinished heads of princesses and of Nefertiti, Akhenaton's beautiful wife.

FIRST FLOOR

Galleries 27 and 32: Displayed here are items of joinery, cattle counts, fishing catches, as well as squads of archers and lance-bearers, which were symbols of the substantial military power of the provincial princes. The models from the tombs of Chancellor Meketre and Prince Mesehti date from the 11th Dynasty.

Gallery 56 (Royal Mummy Room): In 1994 an important position was given to the carefully restored remains of a number of high-ranking personages from ancient Egypt. Laid out behind

Star Attraction

• Egyptian Museum

The last dig
The collection of the Egyptian museum is enormous. Allowing one minute for each exhibit in the museum, it would take more than nine months to see everything. And there is more. In the basement of the museum are more than 40,000 objects, many uncatalogued, piled one on top of the other. Archaeologists often joke that the basement is the last important dig in Egypt.

The mummy of Tuthmosis II

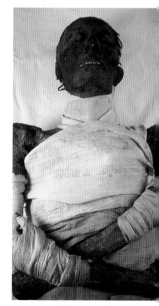

Map on page 25

Fayyum portraits

In room 14 in the Eastern wing of the Egyptian Museum are the delightful life-like 'Fayyum Portraits', found by Sir Flinders Petrie at Hawara. The portraits of the faces were painted in encaustic, pigments mixed in molten wax, and then glued onto the Greco-Roman mummies (AD100–250). The portraits are so realistic you get the impression they are staring at you in a sort of gentle amazement.

The gold mummy masks of Yhuya and Yuya

special glass windows are the remains of such famous pharaohs as Tuthmosis II, Sethos I and Ramesses II; the climate inside simulates that of the rock tombs in the Valley of the Kings.

★★★The Treasure of Tutankhamun

The sensational discovery in 1922 of the undesecrated tomb of Tutankhamun made this insignificant pharaoh, who was only about 18 when he died around 1340BC, famous throughout the world.

Gallery 8: This gallery contains the four gilt shrines covered with texts that once enclosed the coffins and stone sarcophagus of Tutankhamun. The sarcophagus can still be seen in the tomb in the Valley of the Kings.

Gallery 4: The most famous gallery in the museum contains the two outer mummy-shaped coffins, made of gold hammered over wooden frames, the innermost coffin of solid gold, Tutankhamun's world-famous solid-gold portrait mask, and several items of jewellery. The cobra and vulture emblem on the solid gold inner coffin is a symbol of royal dignity. One particularly magnificent exhibit is the gilt throne of Tutankhamun. Studded with emeralds, it features a number of animal likenesses. The seat is flanked by two lions' heads, and the arms are shaped like snakes. On the back is a family portrait: Tutankhamun with his wife Anchesenamun, seen here oiling his body, with the broad rays of the sun in the background.

PICNIC GARDENS

To continue the tour from Maydan al-Tahrir, walk from the square across the Tahrir Bridge to the south, to reach Gazirah Island. Pass the **Cairo Opera House ❸**, across the Nile from Maydan al-Tahrir, and visit its Modern Art Gallery. Then head north along the Andalusian Gardens beside the Nile.

The park derives its name from its copy of the Lion Fountain at the Alhambra in Granada, Spain. The 100-ton obelisk of Ramesses II came from Tanis in the Nile Delta. Beyond the obelisk, take the next street to the left for the **Cairo Tower** (al-Burg) ❹. This cylindrical structure is faced with a concrete net which opens out at the top in the shape of a lotus flower. A lift goes up to the revolving restaurant and observation deck; in clear weather there's a superb view, extending all the way to the Nile Delta and the Pyramids.

Star Attractions
● **Treasure of Tutankhamun**
● **Museum of Islamic Art**

TOUR 2

This walk begins in the southern part of the Islamic Old City at the Maydan Ahmad Mahir, the location of the ★★**Museum of Islamic Art** ❺ (open 9am–4pm). The collection here, unique in the world, comprises 62,000 exhibits and features Islamic masterpieces from many different epochs and countries. It provides a complete overview of artistic development since Islamisation, and is a good place to start before visiting the monuments of Islamic Cairo and beyond.

To do justice to the collection you will need at least a day. Otherwise stick to the highlights. The artefacts are arranged by type, rather than chronology, so it is not important where you start. Highlights include elaborate mashrabiya woodwork; the beautiful door of the Mosque of Sayyida Zeinab; the Islamic weaponry; and a small collection of illuminated manuscripts and fine

Below: geometric decoration in the Islamic Museum
Bottom: the New Cairo Opera House

Map on page 25

Below: a Cairo courtyard
Bottom: in the Gayer-Anderson Museum

Qur'ans – once the property of King Farouk. The oldest of the parchment fragments, which date back to the 8th century AD, were brought to the King of Nubia by the Abbasid prefect Moussa. Upstairs, there is a good collection of carpets and textiles from all over the Islamic world.

HISTORIC MOSQUES

Walk east along Sharia Ahmed Maher, past the beautifully restored Bab Zuwaylah, and continue along Darb al-Ahmar with its many fine mosques, before turning right at the end, at Bab al-Wazir. This street along the citadel walls leads to Maydan Salah ad-Din and the ★★★ ✍ **Mosque-Madrasa of Sultan Hassan ❻** (open winter 9am–5pm, summer 8am–6pm), a masterpiece of Mamluk architecture financed with monies expropriated from victims of the plague of 1348. Its main minaret is 81m (266ft) high – the tallest in Cairo. According to records, four minarets were built at first, but one collapsed killing 300 people.

The most magnificent part of the mosque is the courtyard, with such perfect proportions that the walls seemingly soar up into the sky. The mosque also functioned as a madrasa (school), and each vaulted recess was dedicated to a college of the four legal rites of Sunni Islam. At the back of the prayer hall is a somber mausoleum where Sultan Hassan's two young sons are buried (the remains of the Sultan himself were never recovered after his as--sassination). During the conflicts of the amirs, the roof of the mosque provided the ideal vantage point from which to bombard the Citadel with catapults and cannon.

Return to the Maydan and turn right, then right again onto Sharia Saliba until you reach the ★★★ **Mosque of Ahmed Ibn Tulun ❼** (open daily 8am–5pm). Built in AD876–9, this is one of the oldest and largest mosques in Cairo, and in its simplicity and grandeur it is a unique example of Islamic architecture. Legend has it that Ahmed Ibn Tulun, the son of a Turkish slave and later the founder of the Tulunid dynasty, built the mosque; (the style is Mesopotamian), with a classic congregational courtyard, brick piers, wood carved decoration and an unusual spiral minaret.

Next door to the mosque is the ★★★ **Gayer-Anderson Museum** ❽ (open daily 8am–4pm). Also known as the Beit al-Kretliya, this 16th–17th century house was the home of British Army medical officer Robert Gayer-Anderson, who collected paintings, furniture, glassware, carpets, silks and embroidered Arab costumes.

MIGHTY FORTRESS

Back on Maydan Salah ad-Din, walk south along the walls of the Citadel until you reach the entrance on Sharia Salah Salem, at Bab al-Jabal. Cairo's ★★ **Citadel** ❾ (open daily 8am–5pm) was commissioned in 1176 by Salah ad-Din (Saladin), who repelled the Crusaders on their way to Mecca. Upon its completion 31 years later, it became the mightiest fortress in the Islamic world. Built on the only piece of high ground between the River Nile and the Muqattam Hills, the fortress was considered impregnable. In 1824, however, it was all but destroyed by an explosion.

Muhammad Ali, father of modern Egypt, had palaces and mosques built above the ruins. Six years later the Ottoman-style **Alabaster Mosque**

Star Attractions
● Mosque of Ahmed Ibn Tulun
● Mosque of Sultan Hassan
● Citadel

Unfair deal
The elaborate French clock in the courtyard of the Muhammad Ali Mosque was a present from the French king Louis-Philippe in 1846. It looks somewhat incongruous here and has long stopped working, but the obelisk that the Pasha gave in return still stands in all its glory in the centre of the Place de la Concorde in Paris.

Looking out from the Citadel

Map on page 25

Al-Azhar Park

A city with one of the lowest ratios of green space in the world has now, to the relief of locals and visitors alike, been transformed with the creation of the 30-hectare (74-acre) Al-Azhar Park (open daily 10am–10pm in winter, 10am–midnight in summer; small admission charge) near the Citadel. The daunting project included the excavation and restoration of the 12th-century Ayyubid wall, and the installation of fountains and a lake with fantastic views over the city. There are several good cafés and restaurants open until late.

(also known as the Mosque of Muhammad Ali Pasha) was completed. With a large central cupola and two 80-metre (262-ft) high minarets, it is one of Cairo's major landmarks.

The **al-Haram Palace** was built by Muhammad Ali as a private harem; today it is a military museum. South of the Mosque is **Gawharah Palace**, where in 1811 Muhammad Ali invited 470 Mamluk leaders to dinner, only to have them all put to death.

The view across the city from the Citadel is magnificent, and in good weather extends as far as the Pyramids. The **Haqa Fatma cannon** up here is very popular with photographers; in Ramadan, its unmistakable sound marks the end of the daily fast. Nearby, **Al-Azhar Park** now serves as the city's much needed green lung (*see box*).

In the shadow of the Muhammed Ali Mosque is the Citadel's only surviving Mamluk structure, the **Mosque of an-Nasir Muhammed**. The once rich interior was stripped by the Ottomans, but the minarets remain covered in glazed turquoise tiles imported from Tabriz (Iran).

TOUR 3

In AD969, the Fatimid Gawhar al-Siqilli decided to build a Shiite religious centre: ★★ **Al-Azhar Mosque University** ❿ (open daily 8am–6pm) is probably the oldest institution of advanced learning in Islam. Now Sunnite, it is the highest religious authority in Egypt, and an important spiritual centre of the Muslim world. Some 120,000 men and women are taught by 6,000 lecturers, sometimes in the mosque itself. The Sheikh al-Azhar is the ultimate theological authority for Egyptian Muslims.

Al-Azhar (literally 'the blooming') has been extended several times in its history, and only a few sections of the building still date from the Fatimid era. The domes of the mosque were among the first of their kind in Egypt.

From the Al-Azhar Mosque take the underpass beneath the main road and you will emerge on the opposite side at the **Mosque of Sayyidna**

Studying at the al-Azhar Mosque

al-Husayn. In the eyes of the Shiites, Husayn is the greatest martyr of Islam; the Sunnites see him mainly as one of the sons of the Khalif Ali and as the grandson of the Prophet. This mosque was consecrated to Husayn in 1792. After Husayn fell at the battle of Kerbala (Iraq) in 680, his friends apparently sewed his head into a green cloth. In 1153 a head, ostensibly that of Husayn, was brought to Cairo and placed beneath today's tomb. Pilgrims walk around the enormous silver *mashrabiyyah* screen that surrounds Husayn's grave and pray for release from pain and suffering. Non-Muslims are sometimes allowed inside the building.

BUSY BAZAAR

West of the mosque is the start of the ★★★ **Khan al-Khalili Bazaar** ⑪, founded as a *souk*, or Arab market, in 1382. It consisted originally of one enormous warehouse, or *khan*, which was then extended. The bazaar was a meeting-point for caravans from as far away as India. Silk, precious stones and saffron were just a few of the goods that changed hands. The heavy aroma of perfume mingles with the smell of spice, and the marketplace is full of traders and souvenir salesmen selling papyrus, leather goods, hookahs and all sorts of knick-knacks.

Star Attractions
● **Al-Azhar Mosque**
University
● **Khan al-Khalili Bazaar**

Below: Al-Husayn Mosque
Bottom: bazaar goods

Take your eyes off the merchandise for a while to admire the architecture itself: the arches and some of the courtyards are magnificent.

TOUR 4

This is a walk around *Misr al-Qadima*, or Old Cairo, inhabited mainly by Christian Copts and enclosed by the walls of the Roman Fortress of Babylon. The quarter can be reached by taxi or via the subway (Mari Girgis stop).

Start this tour down the road at the ★**Mosque of Amr Ibn al-As ⓬**, the Arab general who brought Islam to Egypt in the 7th century. In the course of its history it was destroyed by fire (1168) and then by an earthquake (1303). Most of the present facade dates from the renovations in 1977. Inside, 200 of the original 365 pillars still remain; they were 'borrowed' from Coptic, Byzantine and Roman structures. At the tomb of Amr's son, Abdallah, are two pillars with deep impressions in their surface caused, so the legend goes, by the kisses of the sick as they prayed to be cured of their afflictions. Walking back towards the Mari Girgis Station, note the modern Suq al-Fustat (open daily 8am–4pm) on the corner with excellent craft stalls and workshops.

Fustat

The ruins of Fustat, the city founded by the first Muslim conquerors, lie behind the mosque of Amr Ibn al-As and the fortress of Babylon. A guardian can show you around the excavations, but it is hard to imagine now what the city must have looked like. In 1168 it was one of the wealthiest cities in the world, with a water supply and sanitation systems never seen in Europe. Around 200,000 people lived in Fustat, and when threatened by the crusader force of the King of Jerusalem, the Fatimid minister ordered the city to be burned rather than surrender, and it did burn for 54 days.

Sleepy cat at the Babylon fortress

ROMAN BABYLON

Walk straight on, and almost opposite the station is the **Roman Fortress of Babylon**. There have been various attempts to explain how the Euphrates name "Babylon" came to Egypt; the Roman Historian Diodorus Siculus thought that prisoners of war from the Euphrates brought it with them. They arrived as slaves in 2000BC, then rebelled and built a fortress.

A flight of steps next door to the Monastery of St George leads into the Coptic quarter of Kasr esh-Sham. To the left of the street is the Coptic convent of St George. The circular church has a chapel which contains relics of St George, and a 'chain-wrapping ritual' is performed here in memory of the saint's persecution.

At the end of the alley, below today's street level, is the Orthodox ★ **Church of St Sergius** ⓭ (open daily 8am–4pm). It is built over a crypt in which the Holy Family is thought to have once sought refuge during their flight into Egypt, and is consecrated to the martyrs Sergius and Bucchus, two Roman officials murdered in Syria in AD303. The iconostasis (screen separating the sanctuary from the nave) is worthy of note. The ivory carvings depict the story of Christ's birth, and the Feeding of the Five Thousand. St Sergius is a prototype for many Coptic churches. A festival to commemorate the Holy Family's stay here is held on 1 June every year.

MARTYRED DAUGHTER

A short distance away is the little **Church of St Barbara**. Barbara was a young woman who tried to convert her father to Christianity and was duly put to death by him.

A little further on is the **Ben Ezra Synagogue** (open daily 8am–5pm). It stood on ancient Jewish land, and in the 12th century it was consecrated as a synagogue by Ben Ezra, a rabbi from Jerusalem. According to Jewish tradition this is where the prophet Jeremiah preached in the 6th century BC, but the Copts believe it to be the spot where Baby Moses was found in a basket.

Below: the Mosque of Amr Ibn al-As
Bottom: the Ben Ezra Synagogue

Mary on the Nile
It is generally believed that the Holy Family – Mary, the infant Jesus and Joseph her husband – spent four years moving around Egypt. They crossed into Sinai, and then crossed to the Nile from where they went south along the river to Asyut. In many places where they are believed to have rested or lived the Copt built churches and monasteries.

Coptic Museum embroidery

COPTIC MUSEUM

Return to St Sergius now, and go through the gardens that lead to the ★★ **Coptic Museum** ⓴ (open daily 9am–5pm; no cameras). This unique museum of Coptic art was founded in 1910. The 29 halls contain fascinating exhibits documenting Coptic art from AD300 until around AD1000. The building itself is a conglomeration of interesting items: the doors, balconies, and window frames are all from old Coptic houses and churches. The exhibits inside the museum are organised according to the materials used: the new wing contains stone, metal, manuscripts and tapestry work, and the old wing wood, clay and glasswork.

Room 2 illustrates how pharaonic symbols slowly developed into Christian ones, including the ankh into the cross and Isis suckling her son Horus into the image of the Virgin Mary. **Room 3** has a wonderful niche from the Bawit monastery in Upper Egypt, with a representation of Christ with the Riders of the Apocalypse. On the opposite wall is a colourful fresco of Angels carrying Jesus. From the Monastery of St Jeremiah at Saqqarah is the earliest stone pulpit (**Room 6**) and a fresco in which the Virgin Mary is identified with the goddess Isis. The 11th-century pastel-coloured fresco of Fayoum (**Room 9**) shows Adam and Eve before and after the Fall. Climbing the stairs to the First Floor, note in **Room 10** a case with ostraca and papyri including the Gnostic Gospels of Nag Hammadi, translated from Greek into Coptic. The Copts were excellent weavers, and so much becomes clear when looking at the exquisite detail on the textiles in the same room.

SUSPENDED CHURCH

Walk across the garden and to the left find a gate leading to the ★ **Hanging Church** (Al Mu'allaqa or 'The Suspended'), so called because it was built on top of the Roman bastions which is still visible at the back of the church. Ascend the steep stairway to enter the 7th-century church, built like an upturned ark. The interior is splendid, with superb 13th-century panels inlaid with bone and ivory hiding the three *haikals* (altars), fine icons and a carved marble pulpit.

RIVER GAUGE

Now walk towards the Nile, and along the bank to the north, then cross over to Rawdah Island via the ornate metal footbridge.

A small kiosk with a conical roof on the southern tip of the island contains the **Nilometer** ⑮ (open daily 10am–5pm). The level of the Nile has played an important role in Egypt since pharaonic times. The water level always had to be above 7m (23ft) in order to irrigate the fields properly, and anything below that level meant certain drought and famine.

This Nilometer dates from AD861, and was used by the Arabs to calculate how much tax to levy: high water meant high taxes, and vice versa. It's possible to climb down into the basin here. In the 10th Coptic month (August), the prettiest maiden in the city was married to Father Nile during the fertility festival held at the time of the Nile floods.

The ticket for the Nilometer gives entry to the **Manastirli Palace**, a Rococo palace from the 1800s, now the Umm Kulthoum Museum celebrating the popular singer Umm Kulthoum, known as 'The Lady', who died in 1975.

Star Attraction
● Coptic Museum

Below: stained glass window in the Coptic Museum
Bottom: the Nilometer

Map
below

2: Giza, Saqqarah and Memphis

If taking a taxi to the **★★★ Pyramids** (open daily 8am–sunset for the plateau, tickets from 8am to enter the Pyramids) from central Cairo, say 'Funduq Mena House' to the driver, because the little kiosk for the Pyramids is just behind the hotel (separate entrance fees for site, the Pyramids and the Solar Boat Museum). Some guides offering their services ask for a lot of money, as do camel drivers.

THE PYRAMIDS OF GIZA

The Greek historian Herodotus admired the Pyramids, and they have fascinated visitors ever since. The largest structures of the antique world, they

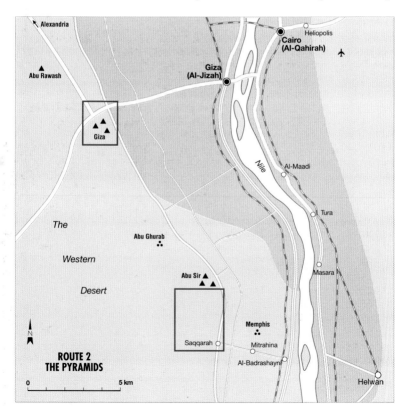

stand on a plateau on the edge of the Western Desert where, according to ancient Egyptian belief, the Kingdom of the Dead began. The Pyramids themselves are built of granite and limestone. The use of limestone may appear unusual in something built to last for eternity, but there was a practical reason: the limestone quarries were not far away, while the granite ones were 800km (500 miles) distant. The fact that granite was used for the burial chambers extended the construction period by an extra 20 years.

THE CONSTRUCTION

Since block and tackle had not yet been invented, one theory goes that the blocks were pulled on skids up huge ramps made of clay bricks. Another more likely theory suggests that the ramps were built in a kind of spiral around the structure as it grew. Roughly 2,300,000 blocks averaging 2.5 tons were used, for the Great Pyramid alone. When the Pyramids had been built, they were faced with limestone from top to bottom and the ramps were removed.

CHEOPS

★★★ **The Great Pyramid [A]**, also known as the Pyramid of Cheops, or Khufu (tickets to go inside on sale from 8am) now stands 137m (449ft) high but was originally 140m (459ft). The archaeologist Flinders Petrie discovered that the relationship of its height to its circumference is amazingly close to that of the radius of a circle to its circumference. Were the ancient Egyptians familiar with *pi* (3.14159265358979323846…)?

Its sides face the four cardinal points, and the entrance is on the north side. The blocks are so well cut that it is almost impossible to insert anything in the joints. Cheops had it built in around 2560BC. There are actually three burial chambers that are thought to mark changes in the plan of the whole building: one is 38m (125ft) below ground, a second one lies at the centre of the structure, and the third one is situated a little higher, at the top of a passageway known as the Grand Gallery. This

Star Attraction
● The Great Pyramid

Pyramid shows
The best time to visit the Giza Pyramids is early in the morning or late afternoon to avoid the crowds. You can rent a horse from one of the nearby stables *(see page 116)* and watch the sun set behind the pyramids. A *son et lumière* show is held several times a day in many languages (including English) at a theatre beside the Sphinx. For information tel: (02) 3386 3469.

The pyramids of Mykerinos, Chephren and Cheops

Map
below

👁 **A great wall**
Napoleon's men calculated that with the stones of the three pyramids of Giza, a wall 3 metres (10ft) high and 30cm (1ft) thick could be built around the whole of France.

third chamber contains a lidless sarcophagus of red granite, and above it are five so-called relieving chambers, cleverly designed to take the weight of the upper part of the pyramid, to prevent it from crushing the burial chamber.

SAILING INTO THE AFTERWORLD

A building that resembles a ship and lies on the south side of the Great Pyramid contains the ★★ **Solar Boat [B]** (open daily 9am–5pm, 4pm in winter). It was found in 1954 underneath the paving surrounding the Great Pyramid. Recovering the boat from the pit in which it rested presented a great many problems, and it wasn't until 1982 that the boat went on display.

Five such boats were constructed for Cheops to accompany him through the afterworld, and another was found but remains unexcavated. An analysis of the mud has shown that the boat, made of cedar wood, was once used on the Nile.

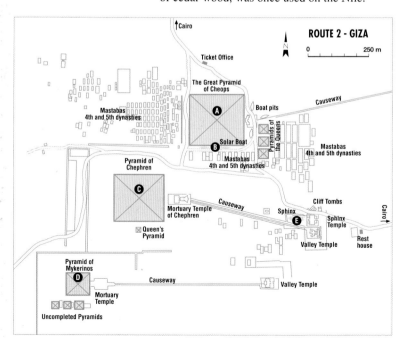

ROUTE 2 - GIZA

↑Cairo

Ticket Office

0   250 m

The Great Pyramid of Cheops

Boat pits

Causeway

Mastabas
4th and 5th dynasties

A

Solar Boat
B

Pyramids of the Queens

Mastabas
4th and 5th dynasties

Mastabas
4th and 5th dynasties

Pyramid of Chephren

C

Mortuary Temple of Chephren

Causeway

Sphinx

Cliff Tombs

Sphinx Temple

E

Queen's Pyramid

Valley Temple

Rest house

Cairo→

Pyramid of Mykerinos

D

Causeway

Valley Temple

Mortuary Temple

Uncompleted Pyramids

To the southwest of the Great Pyramid of Cheops lies the ★★★**Pyramid of Chephren [C]**. Although it looks larger than the Great Pyramid it is actually smaller, and only appears so big because it is situated slightly higher. It still has a small amount of its limestone casing near the top. The traditional pyramid complex of pyramid, mortuary temple and valley temple can be seen clearly here. The pharaoh was mummified in the valley temple.

A 500-m (1,640-ft) long covered causeway leads from the valley temple to the mortuary temple, where prayers and sacrifices were held for the pharaoh. A passageway leads 32m (105ft) inside the pyramid to the burial chamber; the sarcophagus, empty when discovered by Belzoni in 1818, is set into the floor.

Star Attractions
● **Solar Boat**
● **Pyramid of Chephren**
● **Pyramid of Mykerinos**
● **The Sphinx**

The Solar Boat

THE SPHYNX

Southwest of the Pyramid of Chephren is the ★★**Pyramid of Mykerinos [D]**, the third of the Giza pyramids and originally 62–66m (203–216ft) high – only around half as high as that of Chephren. The angle of the sides, as with the other pyramids, is 51 degrees. Walk (or ride) eastwards now, down to ★★**The Sphinx [E]**.

This figure, with the body of a lion and the head of a man, is generally believed to be a portrait statue of Chephren, but some believe it could have been the guardian deity of the necropolis (the Sphinx's nose and beard were shot off for fun by Mamluk soldiers).

Made of soft stone, the statue had been suffering from erosion; a newly added layer of limestone has restored its former glory, but the missing nose and beard were left off deliberately. In front of its paws is a granite stele placed there on the orders of Tuthmosis IV (1423–1417BC), who had a dream in which the statue promised him the throne if he freed it of sand. He did so, and duly became pharaoh.

The Egyptians call the Sphinx by its Arabic name "Abu al-Hol", which means the awesome or terrible one.

Map on page 38

A picnic in the desert

Saqqarah has a small cafe-teria with cold drinks near the Serapeum, but the best thing to do if out for the day, particularly outside the summer season, is to bring your own picnic. Cairenes like to have a picnic in the ruins of the Monastery of Jeremiah just off the parking area, where there is some shade, but if it is not too hot it might be more romantic to have it in the desert, with views on the Step Pyramid.

SAQQARAH AND MEMPHIS

After visiting the Giza pyramids head along the canal to Saqqarah. The most comfortable way is to organise a daytrip through a travel agency, but it is easy enough to hire a taxi for the day (agree on a price beforehand).

The road follows the canal to ★★★ **Saqqarah** (open daily 8am–4pm), a vast cemetery where the royalty and nobility were buried for more than 3000 years during the Old Kingdom. Before entering the site, be sure to visit the new Imhotep Museum beside the ticket office. There are many interesting items, including statues, mummies and wooden models released from the Egyptian Museum in Cairo.

BURIAL SITE

The famous ★★★ **Step Pyramid [A]** here was built for King Zoser by his chief of works, Imhotep, in around 2665BC, and was the first monumental stone structure in the world. Instead of bricks, Imhotep used limestone, and placed six 60-m (197-ft) high steps above a square ground plan measuring 110m (361ft) by 121m (397ft). The pyramid was meant to represent a kind of ladder by which the king could ascend into heaven. The burial chamber lies at the centre of a labyrinth covering several floors.

The Step Pyramid was part of a large complex surrounded by a limestone wall measuring 500m by 308m (1,640ft by 1,010ft), part of which has been rebuilt near the entrance.

Next to the pyramid is the **Heb Sed Court**, where every seven years a festival was held to renew the king's vitality. Further on are the **Houses of North and South**, shrines of Upper and Lower Egypt.

To the southwest is the ★★ **Pyramid Complex of Unas [B]**. The walls of the burial chamber are of particular interest. Inscribed and painted blue, they show part of the Pyramid texts. These are the oldest religious texts in Egypt.

SAQQARAH

0   500 m

Abu Sir

Camel track to Pyramids of Giza

Graves

Mastaba of Ti **[D]**

Serapeum

Pyramid of Teti

Pyramid of Userkef

Step Pyramid **[A]**

Pyramid Complex of Unas **[B]**   **[C]** Causeway

Mastaba of Idut

Mastaba of Idut

Pyramid of Horum Sekhemkhet

Monastery of St Jeremiah

Kiosk

ROYAL TOMBS

The site at Saqqarah contains several ancient Egyptian oblong tombs known as *mastabas*. To the east of the Pyramid of Unas is the ★★**Mastaba of Idut [C]**. Idut, a princess of the 5th Dynasty, was probably a daughter of Unas. Her tomb was originally planned for a prince named Ihui. Five of the 10 chambers of the *mastaba* are decorated with colourful reliefs, showing hunting and fishing scenes, dancers at a funeral, and the princess in a boat. The largest *mastaba* in Saqqarah belonged to ★★**Mereruka**. The 32 rooms are decorated with lively wall paintings depicting the Vizier Mereruka hunting and overseeing the farming. Nearby are the *mastabas* of two other viziers, Kagemni and Ankh-Ma-Hor, with lifelike depictions of toe surgery and circumcision. Closer towards the rest house is the splendid 5th-Dynasty double ★★**Mastaba of Akhti-Hotep and Ptah-hotep**, a vizier and his son who was a high priest, with some of the most exquisite Old Kingdom reliefs. There are detailed scenes of musicians and children's games, and you can see how the different stages of the decoration were done.

Northwest of the rest house is the ★★★**Mastaba of Ti [D]**, containing one of the finest 5th-Dynasty reliefs ever discovered. The complex is entered through a columned portico; the walls on each

Star Attractions
● **Saqqarah's pyramids and tombs**

Below: statue in the Imhotep Museum
Bottom: Step Pyramid

Map on page 38

A long line of pyramids
A long line of more than 80 pyramids were built along the Nile between Giza and Al-Fayyum. Many have crumbled or all but disappeared, but pyramid fans can still visit a few. Between Giza and Saqqarah are the Pyramids of Zawiyet al-Aryan; South Saqqarah has a few and further south are the Pyramids of Dahshur (now open to the public), Hawara, Al-Lahun, Al-Lisht and Maydum.

A sphinx at Memphis

side bear the name and titles of Ti, who was an overseer and high official. Magnificent reliefs in the courtyard depict storks, cranes and doves, and the inner chamber contains some fascinating scenes of agricultural life.

Continue along the canal road and then take the first turning on the left in the direction of Mitrahina. This is the site of ★ **Memphis** (open daily 8am–5pm), the capital of the Old Kingdom, founded around 3000BC by the legendary King Menes; it lay on the exact border between Upper and Lower Egypt.

The ruins give little impression of the gigantic city, with palaces, temples, parks and fountains, that once stood on this site. Memphis was a cult-centre for the god Ptah, who was the creator of the gods and the world, and the temple of Ptah was the most important building in town. The temples of Ptah and other gods are in ruins now; most of the stone was taken to Cairo and used for other structures. The houses and palaces were built in mud brick and have also long since disappeared. All that is left is the enormous limestone figure of the young Ramesses II, well worth a visit. Its twin used to stand on the square in front of Ramesses Station, but pollution took its toll.

PHARAONIC VILLAGE

Another enjoyable excursion from Cairo is **Dr Ragab's Pharaonic Village** (open 9am–9pm; winter 9am–5pm, tel: 02-3571 8675), on St Jacob's Island, 3 Shaila al-Bahr al-Aazam in Giza.

Dubbed 'Pharaonic Disneyland' by locals, the reconstructed community simulates everyday life in an ancient Egyptian village: the staff wear the clothes of that time and they work as the ancient Egyptians did. The houses of noblemen and peasants can be visited, and there are boat trips 'through the dynasties' along a canal.

The temple and sacred lake here are especially magnificent, and the landscape, with lotus blooms and fig trees, is colourful. There is also a good replica of the tomb of Tutankhamun from the Valley of the Kings.

3: Alexandria

Alexandria, the 'pearl of the Mediterranean' and the second-largest city in Egypt, has changed a lot since it was founded by Alexander the Great. *Al-Iskandariyyah*, as this metropolis of 5 million people is known today, was the most important harbour in the entire Mediterranean. It imported not only goods from Greece and Italy but also the lifestyle and attitudes of those countries. Alexandria is the most cosmopolitan of Egypt's cities; it is also the Cairenes' most popular holiday destination.

During the 1920s many of Europe's free-thinkers and dilettantes came to Alexandria to find new creativity, attracted by its image as a city open

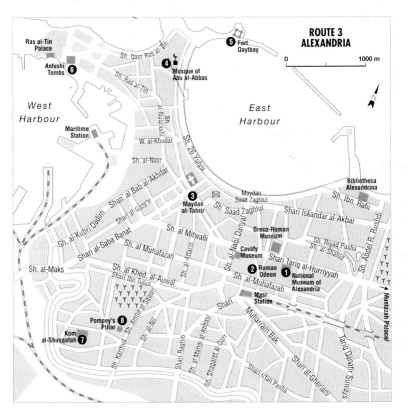

Map on page 45

Underwater discoveries
Some spectacular discoveries were made in the 1990s by diving archaeologists. Near Fort Qaytbey they discovered thousands of blocks and some statues from the ancient Pharos, some of which are on display at the Roman Odeon. In the Eastern Harbour they have found remains of the submerged royal quarters of Cleopatra. The Egyptian government have plans for the world's first underwater museum, where visitors can walk through Plexiglass tunnels to admire the submerged monuments, but this will certainly take time and a lot of money.

The Corniche

to all manner of men and ideas. While its former glory has now been replaced by crumbling facades, Alexandria certainly fits Lawrence Durrell's description of it as 'the capital of nostalgia'.

ANCIENT HISTORY

Shortly after the city's foundation in 332BC, Alexander's successors turned it into a centre of trade and education. Strabo, Euclid and other scholars, philosophers and scientists all drew inspiration here. It was in Alexandria during the 1st century BC that Cleopatra courted first Julius Caesar and then his successor Mark Antony, who later committed suicide with her here. Unfortunately nothing remains today of the enormous Library of Alexandria built by Demetrios, which once contained one million books, but a new library opened its doors in 2002.

The great lighthouse, the Pharos of Alexandria – pride of the ancient city and one of the Seven Wonders of the World – no longer exists either. It collapsed for good in 1307.

It was from Alexandria that the conversion of Egypt to Christianity began during the 1st century, and here that the Roman emperor Diocletian began the persecution of the Christians by ordering the destruction of the city in AD295. Cairo's rise to prominence robbed Alexandria of its importance, and it only experienced a late Renaissance at the beginning of the 19th century under Muhammad Ali.

SIGHTS

As not much remains of ancient Alexandria, the best place to get a feeling of its splendour is at the ★★★**National Museum of Alexandria** ❶ (110 Tariq al-Hurriyyah; open daily 9am–5pm, closed Fri noon for prayer). Set in a fine Italianate villa, this is the latest addition to Alexandria's spread of museums. It illustrates the city's long history with well-displayed and labelled artefacts assimiliated from several of the city's other great museums (including the Greco-Roman Museum and the Naval Museum at Qaytbay's fort. The National Museum is laid out chronologically over three floors, with panels alongside the exhibits to provide an useful running commentary. The basement is devoted to the pharaonic period; the ground floor to the Greco-Roman period (which includes a sphinx and several other sculptures found in the Eastern Harbour); and the top floor to Coptic, Islamic and modern Alexandria.

ROMAN THEATRE

Ancient Alexandria had two main streets: Canopic Street and the Street of Soma – these still exist as Shari Tariq al-Hurriyyah and Shari al-Nabi Danyal. Not far from where the two streets cross stands the elegant ★ ★ **Roman Odeon** ❷ (open daily 9am–5pm), known as Kom al-Dikka, a theatre with marble seating for 800 people that was only discovered in the 1950s. Further excavations are limited by modern buildings, though nearby excavations have revealed a Roman residential area with houses and shops. Also on display are a few of the statues discovered in underwater excavations in the Eastern Harbour (*see box on page 46*). Archaeologists recently uncovered a Roman villa on the site, named **Villa of the Birds** for its large floor mosaics. The villa is open to the public (with a separate ticket).

Star Attractions
● **National Museum of Alexandria**
● **Roman Odeon**

Below: the Apis Bull
Bottom: the Roman Odeon

Map on page 45

Below: a cluttered and eclectic stall in the bazaar
Bottom: the Abu al-Abbas Mosque

DOWNTOWN ALEXANDRIA

Alexandria gained importance under Muhammad Ali, and his equestrian statue dominates ❸ **May-dan al-Tahrir**, the long square that was at first also named after him. Around the square are the Church of St Mark, the Stock Exchange and the Law Courts. Behind Muhammad Ali the square continues as far as the **Gold Market**, which is far more attractive and better value for money than Cairo's bazaar. Another market tucked away to the south of the jewellery district is full of knick-knacks, material and clothing; tailors can often be seen working away on ancient Singer sewing machines.

The ★**Mosque of Abu al-Abbas** ❹ along Alexandria's sweeping Corniche is the biggest mosque in the city. It was erected in the 18th century over the grave of Abu al-Abbas al-Mursi (1219–87), a Muslim holy man from Andalusia. Renovated in 1944, it is an exquisite work of Islamic architecture; the filigree decoration of the domes and minaret is particularly fine.

At the end of the bay, beyond the flotilla of colourful fishing boats, stands ★**Fort Qaytbay** ❺ (open daily 9am–5pm), built in the 15th century by the sultan Ashraf Qayt Bay using the remains of the famed Pharos of Alexandria. This round-towered fortress is located close to the original site of the ancient lighthouse. The old Pharos

had four tiers, was nearly 120m (394ft) high and stood in a colonnaded court; it was crowned by a 7m (23ft) statue of Poseidon; and the fire at the top could be seen 50km (31 miles) away. After a series of earthquakes, the structure collapsed in 1307. More was discovered after an underwater salvage operation in 1994.

Across the Eastern Harbour rises the ★★ **Bibiliotheca Alexandrina** (www.bibalex.org; open Sun–Thur 11am–6.30pm, Fri–Sat 3–6.30pm), a new library and cultural centre on Alexandria's Corniche. Built by the Egyptian government with the help of UNESCO and the Gulf States, the library is dedicated to recapturing the spirit of ancient Alexandria's much-famed library. The modern library will eventually hold 8 million books, mainly in French, English and Arabic – though its strength lies in its collection of around 50,000 manuscripts. Seven research centres are located here, including a centre for calligraphy and a centre for Mediterranean and Alexandrian studies. The whole complex has become a major cultural hub in the city, with Egypt's best concert hall, a children's library, a Science Museum, a Planetarium and the Alexandrina Archaeological Museum all close by. The latter houses finds unearthed during the construction of the library.

Star Attractions
● **Bibliotheca Alexandrina**
● **Kom al-Shuqqafah catacombs**

> **Literary Alexandria**
> Perhaps more than any other city in Egypt, Alexandria has inspired many great writers. EM Forster was so intrigued by the city that he wrote a guidebook to the city, *Alexandria, a History and a Guide*. Lawrence Durrell lived here only two and a half years during the war, but he really brings the city and that time to life in his wonderful *The Alexandria Quartet*. But no one lived, loved and suffered Alexandria more than the Greek poet Constantine Cavafy in his *Collected Poems*.

The Kom al-Shuqqafah catacombs

OTHER SIGHTS

The ★ **Anfushi Tombs** ❻, cut out of the limestone east of the al-Tin Palace (1834), date from the 2nd century BC and have Roman additions. The stucco is painted to resemble marble, alabaster and tiles – a fine example of Greco-Egyptian *trompe l'oeil*.

The catacombs of ★★ **Kom al-Shuqqafah** ❼ (open daily 9am–4pm) date from the 2nd century AD. They form the largest Christian necropolis in Egypt (of the three levels, two are now submerged beneath groundwater). The burial chamber contains statues of Sobek and Anubis, showing the typical Alexandrian blend of styles, and in a small room nearby are some burial niches.

The 26-metre (85-ft) marble column known as **Pompey's Pillar** ❽ has nothing to do with Pom-

Map on page 45

Sweet things
For lost grandeur in Alexandria there are no better places than the old patisseries. Hang out on the terrace like Cavafy and Durrell did and watch the world go by, or meet a lover over a cup of tea with pastries like the Egyptians do. The best ones are Athineos on Maydan Saad Zaghlul, Baudrot with a garden at 23 Sharia Saad Zaghlul, and the popular terraces of Trianon, also on Maydan Saad Zaghlul.

Outside the Trianon café

pey. It was raised in honour of Diocletian around AD300, after he had saved the city from famine – and just before his persecution of the Christians.

For the more recent past of Alexandria, visit the ★ **Cavafy Museum**, (open Tues–Sun 10am–4pm). In a quiet backstreet, the museum is housed in the flat where the Alexandrian-born Greek poet Constantine Cavafy (1863–1933) lived and wrote. It contains his simple furniture, his death mask and many of his books.

ROYAL RESIDENCE

Further east, where the Corniche bends away from the sea, is the **Muntazah Palace** and park, built by Abbas II as his summer residence and restored by King Fuad. The grounds cover a surface area of 141 hectares (338 acres). The main palace is a combination of Turkish and Florentine styles; the central tower is a copy of the one on Florence's Palazzo Vecchio. The park becomes especially animated on Fridays and public holidays during the summer, when music groups perform, and locals come to picnic and take their siestas on the king's rather thin lawns.

DESERT BATTLEFIELD

One interesting excursion from Alexandria is the World War II battlefield of **Al-Alamayn**, which lies 110km (68 miles) outside the city. Between 23 October and 4 November 1942, over 80,000 soldiers died near Al-Alamayn during the famous battle between Rommel, the 'Desert Fox', and the 8th Army commanded by generals Montgomery and Alexander. Thousands of war veterans from both sides make the pilgrimage here every year. After this defeat Rommel grew sympathetic to resistance forces within Germany and was forced to commit suicide on 20 July 1944.

Near the Allied War Cemetery is the **War Museum**, which contains examples of World War II weapons and charts of troop movements during the conflict.

4: In the Garden of Egypt

The metropolis of Cairo is in many ways typical of a modern Egyptian city, but only a few miles out of the capital, the Egypt of the *fellahin* (farm workers) unfolds. The fertility of the Nile Valley, proverbial since antiquity, is breathtaking: lots of orchards, cornfields and groves, and hardly any wooded areas. The *fellahin* irrigate their fields with methods dating back 3,000 years.

This route can be tackled either by car, by shared taxi or by bus, though be sure to check with the tourist office for details of the latest travel restrictions *(see page 53)*.

THE FAYYUM

★ **The Fayyum** is an oasis 101km (63 miles) southwest of Cairo. It is fed directly by the Bahr Yussef, a natural tributary of the Nile, which then flows into **Lake Qarun**. Cairo's fruit and vegetables mostly come from the Fayyum. During the Old Kingdom the Fayyum was a marshy area with several crocodile-infested lakes; the crocodile god Sobek was held in great reverence. It was only when the Ptolemies arrived around the time of Christ's birth that the area was finally made cultivable. Sights in Fayyum town are few, except for the waterwheels and small souk. Most visitors head for Lake Qarun,

Map on page 52

Below and bottom: traditional modes of farming in the Fayyum

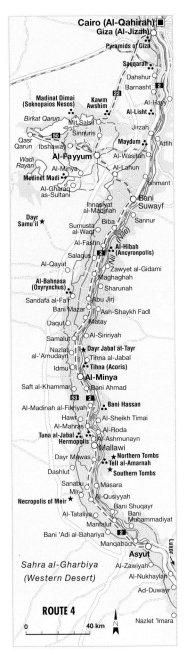

ROUTE 4

0   40 km

to row on the lake, fish or have lunch. On the northwestern edge of the oasis, accessible by taxi or car, lies **Qasr Qarun**, a temple dedicated to Sobek. Further south is **Wadi Rayan** with fresh water lakes and a waterfall, and nearby **Medinet Madi**, a XIIth-Dynasty temple also dedicated to Sobek. Those with a four-wheel drive (and permission) can head for the ancient sites of **Qasr es-Sagha** and **Dimeh es-Siba** in the desert.

Another 111km (69 miles) along the main road is the provincial capital of **Bani Suwayf**, one of the centres of the Egyptian cotton industry, currently in recession.

PAINTED NECROPOLIS

Continue along the western bank of the Nile into Middle Egypt, past cotton fields and sugar-cane plantations, as far as the university town and provincial capital of **Al-Minya**. Carry on beyond the town for a further 29km (18 miles) to ★★**Bani Hassan** (open daily 9am–4pm), an ancient necropolis of 39 tomb-chapels for governors of the 11th and 12th Dynasties. The tomb-chapel of **Kheti**, with wrestling scenes on the walls, is particularly striking; that of **Khnumhotep** is famous for its *Semitic Caravan*, portraying the arrival of 37 traders from the Near East.

A further 8km (5 miles) on (272km/169 miles into the trip) turn off at Ar-Roda/Al-Ashmunayn and follow signs to the sunken capital of **Hermopolis**. This 'city of Hermes' used to be the city of the moon god Thoth, vizier of the gods, usually portrayed as a man with the head of an ibis. The **Temple of Thoth** was commissioned by Amenhotep III, and must have once marked the centre of the city: eight colossal statues of Thoth (4.5m/15ft high) and two giant baboons that once upheld the temple's ceiling were found nearby. More remains of the city's necropolis are at ★★**Tuna al-**

Jabal (open daily 9am–4pm) 6km/4 miles away. In the catacombs mummified baboons and ibises were found, sacred to the god Thoth. The finest tomb belonged to Petosiris, a high priest of Thoth, with colourful scenes from the *Book of Gates* and *Book of the Dead*.

Star Attractions
● Bani Hassan

MONOTHEISTIC HERESY

Another 17km (10 miles) along the main road, on the other side of the Nile, is the ancient site of ★ **Tell al-Amarnah** – there's a ferry link at at-Till. A handful of ruins is all that remains. Akhenaten, formerly Amenhotep III, replaced the official god Amun by the cult of the Aten and worship of the sun disk, the world's first monotheistic religion. He shifted the capital here from Thebes, naming it Akhenaten. Within 12 years it had become a flourishing city. After Akhenaten's death, Tutankhamun, probably his son, broke with his father's cult and re-established the Amun capital of Thebes. The famous bust of Nefertiti, Akhenaten's beautiful wife (in the Egyptian Museum in Berlin) was found during excavations here. The 25 tomb-chapels in the rock are in disrepair but the tomb of Meryre I (No 4), high priest of the Aten, contains paintings showing what the temple of the sun looked like. A further 85km (52 miles) is the provincial capital of Asyut.

Travel restrictions
Travel is still very restricted along the Nile, particularly along the stretch from Cairo to Luxor, as this is where most of the attacks by Islamic fundamentalists have taken place. There are usually no restrictions to travel from Cairo to Al-Fayyum, but further on tourists are allowed to travel only in armed convoys. Check with the tourist office for the departure times of the convoy, and on the current situation. Tourists are not allowed to stay overnight in Middle Egypt.

The Temple of Thoth, Hermopolis

Map
below

5: Luxor, Karnak and Thebes

Luxor, 675km (419 miles) south of Cairo, occupies part of the site of the ancient city of Thebes, and is the oldest and most important tourist destination in Upper Egypt. Ramesses II, Tutankhamun, Seti I, Amenhotep II, Tuthmosis III and Hatshepsut all left massive monuments here. The tourist industry hasn't made Luxor the most relaxing town for visitors – the taxi drivers, coach drivers and traders are far pushier than anywhere else in Egypt.

The distances in Luxor and Karnak can be covered on foot, but it might be more pleasant to hire a horse-drawn carriage or to cycle. Those intending to visit the West Bank, on the other side of the Nile, should hire a taxi or cross on the ferry and rent a bicycle.

The Theban Triad
The temples in Luxor and Karnak are both dedicated to the Theban Triad of the god Amun, his wife Mut and his son Khonsu. Amun later became the state deity as Amun-Re, a fusion with the sun god Re, worshipped as Supreme Creator. The goddess Mut was the Mistress of Heaven and Khonsu was the moon god, sometimes also 'the traveller'.

HISTORY

The pharaohs knew Thebes as *Waset*, the Greeks called it *Thebai* (derived from *ta-ope*, the ancient

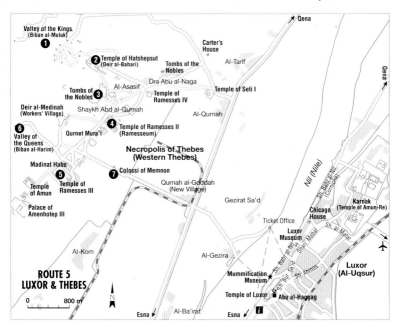

Valley of the Kings (Biban al-Muluk) ❶
❷ Temple of Hatshepsut (Deir al-Bahari)
Tombs of the Nobles
Carter's House
Al-Tarif
Qena
Qena
Dra Abu al-Naga
Al-Asasif
Temple of Seti I
Tombs of ❸ the Nobles
Temple of Ramesses IV
Deir al-Medinah (Workers' Village)
Shaykh Abd al-Qurnah
Al-Qurnah
❻ Valley of the Queens (Biban al-Harim)
Qurnet Mura'i
❹ Temple of Ramesses II (Ramesseum)
Madinat Habu
Necropolis of Thebes (Western Thebes)
❺
❼ Colossi of Memnon
Qurnah al-Goddah (New Village)
Temple of Amun
Temple of Ramesses III
Geziret Sa'd
Nil (Nile)
Palace of Amenhotep III
Ticket Office
Sh. Bahr al-Nil (Corniche)
Sh. al-Matar
Karnak (Temple of Amun-Re)
Chicago House
Luxor Museum
Al-Kom
Al-Gezira
Sh. Bahr al-Nil
Shari Matar
Sh. al-Matar
Sh. Ahmos
Luxor (Al-Uqsur)
ROUTE 5 LUXOR & THEBES
0   800 m
N
Mummification Museum
Temple of Luxor
Abu al-Haggag
Esna
Al-Ba'irat
Esna

Egyptian name for Luxor) and the Arabs named it *Al-Uqsur* ('the palaces'). Luxor owes its rise to prominence to the local god Amun, who was the most important deity in Egypt during the Middle Kingdom. Amun, along with Mut and Khonsu, formed the so-called 'Theban Triad'. Thebes became the centre of power during the New Kingdom, controlling an area that extended from the depths of modern Sudan and Libya.

Star Attraction
● Temple of Luxor

Below: entrance to the Luxor temple
Bottom: Opet festival relief

The Egyptian armies brought back a lot of wealth from their campaigns in Africa and Asia, much of which was used for the embellishment of Thebes and for the upkeep of its priesthood. Successive, ever more powerful New Kingdom pharaohs vied to make a bigger mark on the place.

From Alexander the Great onwards, Luxor lost its political power to Alexandria, but it remained the religious capital for centuries thereafter. It slowly became a sleepy market town, until the late 18th century, when the scholars and archaeologists who came with Napoleon recognised it as the ancient Waset.

LUXOR: EASTERN BANK OF THE NILE

All three religions connected with Egypt are represented in the famous temple on the eastern bank of the Nile. The ★★★ **Temple of Luxor** (open daily 6am–9pm in winter, 10pm in summer, *see map on next page*), built by Amenhotep III and Ramesses II in honour of the gods Amun, Mut and Khonsu, contains an early mosque, and part of it has been used as a church. It was connected to the Temple of Karnak by a 3-km (1.8-mile) **Avenue of Sphinxes**; from the entrance of the temple, it is possible to gain a good impression of just how majestic this must have been.

The **entrance pylon [A]** before the peristyle court depicts the glorious exploits of Ramesses II on its outer face, including scenes from the Battle of Kadesh when the pharaoh beat the Hittites. Only two of the original four seated figures still remain, and neither of the two standing ones.

The reliefs in the **peristyle court [B]** depict a procession. After this comes the **colonnade [C]**,

The Golden Head of Mehit-Weret, Luxor Museum

with a rare work of art dating back to the time of Tutankhamun. The delicately outlined reliefs depict the scenes of the feast of Opet, and at the centre a procession of deities can be seen on their way from the Temple of Karnak to the Temple of Luxor. The streets are lined with people, and dancers and musicians perform; citizens, their hands raised to heaven, greet the gods.

Pass through the courtyard [**D**], entrance hall [**E**] and antechamber [**F**] to arrive at the sanctuary [**G**]. In the neighbouring **Birth Room**, reliefs emphasise the divine origin of Amenhotep III.

LUXOR MUSEUM

The excellent ★★**Luxor Museum** (open daily 9am–1pm, 5–10pm; 9am–1pm, 4–9pm in winter; extra admission fee for Statue Hall) containing finds from Luxor and Thebes, was opened in 1975. Its treasures include the gilt head of the cow-goddess Mehit-Weret, with leather horns and eyes of lapis lazuli, and several funerary gifts found in the tomb of Tutankhamun. Don't miss the alabaster sculpture, discovered in 1967, of the crocodile god Sobek with Amenhotep III. The latter had himself immortalised in granite in a variety of poses; he can be seen seated, standing, clenching his fist, and also wearing the blue crown of a warrior pharaoh. Magnificent statues recently discovered in the Temple of Luxor are new to the collection. Also on the Corniche is a small but excellent ★★**Mummification Museum** (open daily 9am–1pm, 5–10pm; 9am–1pm, 4–9pm in winter) explaining the process and history of mummification.

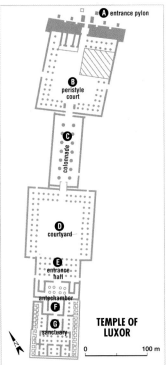

TEMPLE OF LUXOR

Ⓐ entrance pylon

Ⓑ peristyle court

Ⓒ colonnade

Ⓓ courtyard

Ⓔ entrance hall

antechamber

Ⓕ

Ⓖ sanctuary

0   100 m

KARNAK

The 3km (1.8 mile) distance between Luxor and Karnak makes an enjoyable carriage ride, though it is an easy walk and taxis also ply the route. ★★★**Karnak** (open daily 6am–5.30pm in winter, 6pm in summer)

is a unique experience. From the Middle Kingdom onwards, each pharaoh tried to outdo the
preceding one in making Karnak even more magnificent. All this construction activity lasted 2,000
years, during which the kings were not always
respectful of their ancestors' efforts, taking from
the older temples to build new ones. The most
important builders were Tuthmosis I and III,
Queen Hatshepsut, Amenhotep III, Ramesses II
and his father Seti I, the kings of Bubastis and
finally the Ptolemies, who ruled Egypt before the
founding of Rome.

TEMPLE OF AMUN

The Avenue of Sphinxes leads from the Temple
of Luxor to Karnak's great **Temple of Amun**.
Beyond the **entrance pylon [H]** is the ★★ **First
Forecourt [I]**, 103m (338ft) by 84m (275ft), the
largest of any Egyptian temple. There used to be
ten 21-m (69-ft) high columns here, but only the

Star Attractions
- Luxor Museum
- Karnak's temples

Son et lumière
There are *son et lumière*
shows in Karnak every
evening, providing the ideal introduction to this confusing complex of
temples within temples – the light
illuminates what is important, while
the rest is plunged into shadow. Part
of the show takes place in the complex itself, and part at elevated rows
of seating behind the sacred lake (tel:
095-237 2241).

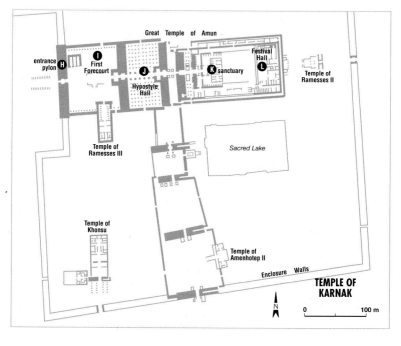

TEMPLE OF KARNAK

Map on page 54

Gods for the people
The Amun precinct in Karnak was accessible only to the priest and royalty, but the people used intermediary deities to transmit their petitions to the Theban Triad. These minor gods had their own shrines known as the Chapels of the Hearing Ear. These small chapels were located at the back of the Temple, but are now mostly in ruin.

middle one remains. To the right is the **Temple of Ramesses III**, which was only later included in the forecourt. It gives an idea of the basic design of every temple, with a forecourt, lifestyle hall and sanctuary. Beyond the second pylon (gateway) is one of the wonders of the antique world, the immense ★★★ **Hypostyle Hall [J]**. It measures 102m (334ft) by 53m (174ft) and contains 134 sandstone columns in 16 rows, forming a symbolic garden. This massive hall with a stone roof was built by Seti I, with decoration by Ramesses II, and is the most striking feature of the temple. The reliefs on the walls and the columns describe the relationship of the pharaohs to the gods.

The third to the sixth pylons lead to the two-chambered granite **sanctuary [K]**. The outer and inner walls are decorated with reliefs showing the pharaoh making sacrifices to the gods. The obelisks were erected by Tuthmosis I and III, the two pink-granite ones by Queen Hatshepsut. One fell down but the other is the tallest standing obelisk in Egypt. Inscriptions reveal that each one was made from a single piece of granite, and gilded with vast amounts of the finest gold.

HUNTING SCENES

Cross a grass-covered area now to reach the ★ **Festival Hall [L]**. The famous royal tablet of Karnak,

The Karnak Temple

showing Tuthmosis carrying out the holy sacrifice in front of 62 of his predecessors (the original can be seen in the Louvre), was discovered in the entrance area of the Temple of Tuthmosis III. The reliefs show the pharaoh out on a hunt. Don't miss the **Botanical Room**, only the bottom section of which survives. Its reliefs form a pictorial catalogue of the plants and animals Tuthmosis brought back from Syria, including sunflowers, goats, falcons and chickens. The complex ends at the eastern gate.

Not far away is the **Sacred Lake**, placed here by Amenhotep III so that the priests could carry out their ritual washing four times a day. The tribune above the lake provides a magnificent view of Karnak to round off the tour. On the way back, next to the great Hypostyle Hall, on the north-south axis of the temple, lies the **Cachette Court** where 17,000 bronze and 800 stone statues were discovered. North of the Temple of Amun is an **Open Air Museum**.

THEBES: WESTERN BANK OF THE NILE

The Nile's western bank is easily reached by taxi across the bridge south of town. Alternatively, you take the ferry opposite the Temple of Luxor and then a taxi on the other side of the river, or rent a bicycle. Some of the tombs have suffered from the moisture caused by visitors and from the High Dam's rising water and may be closed without prior warning. Some, like the fine tomb of Seti I, may never be open to the public again, others open on a rotation basis. Check with the tourist office before setting out to visit.

Admission tickets to all sites on the western bank are sold at the central office near the Colossi of Memnon, not at the monuments. There is an extra charge to visit the tomb of Tutankhamun. Sites are open daily 6am–5pm; minor tombs may close earlier in summer.

SACRED VALLEY

The ★★★ **Valley of the Kings ❶** is sacred to a local goddess, Mertsigir, 'she who loves silence'.

Star Attractions
● Hypostyle Hall
● Valley of the Kings

Below: Ramesses II at Karnak
Bottom: ferry across the Nile

Map on page 54

Below: Valley of the Kings
Bottom: the Tomb
of Tutankhamun

It contains tombs of almost all the pharaohs of the 18th, 19th and 20th Dynasties (1539–1075BC). Ireni, chief of works of Pharaoh Tuthmosis I (18th Dynasty) hoped that a tomb hidden in the rock here would provide much greater protection from tomb-robbers than the Pyramids.

Tuthmosis I was probably the first pharaoh to be buried in this valley, and the mortuary temple was built a long way from the tomb for added safety. This principle was faithfully followed for the next 500 years – but all precautions were in vain. Most tombs were robbed during the lifetime of the deceased pharaohs' successors. In Strabo's time, around AD10, Greek travellers were already able to visit as many as 40 tombs.

TOMB CONSTRUCTION

The architectural principle of the tombs was simple from the start and remained much the same. A passageway was driven down at an angle up to 200m (656ft) into the limestone rock face. The burial chamber was protected from intruders by a series of trapdoors and the main entrance was hidden beneath mounds of earth and rubble. The tombs were decorated with psalms, magic formulae from the *Book of the Dead*, pictures of gods or painted biographies of the deceased.

TUTANKHAMUN

The ★★ **Tomb of Tutankhamun** (No 62) is the most famous tomb in the Valley of the Kings. The boy king replaced Akhenaten's 'heretical' cult of the Aten (the sun disk) with the old cult of Amun – perhaps one reason why the 18-year-old pharaoh's grave was filled with so much gold and jewellery. As Howard Carter, who found the tomb under one of his team's huts, quipped: 'The only remarkable thing about his life was that he died and was buried.'

The tomb formerly contained the four gilt shrines covered with texts that enclosed the coffins and stone sarcophagus of Tutankhamun. The mummy lay in the innermost coffin of solid gold. Tutankhamun's tomb provided the first proof of the immense wealth of the pharaohs – and of the treasures that robbers must have stolen from the tombs of far greater rulers.

A staircase leads to a corridor, and then an antechamber leads to the burial chamber itself. The king's mummified body was enclosed inside three coffins. The middle one, wooden and richly ornamented, remains here in the tomb with the mummy of Tutankhamun inside it; the other coffins, as well as the other treasure, can be seen in the Egyptian Museum in Cairo *(see page 28)*. All three coffins lay inside the quartzite sarcophagus, which can also be seen in the tomb (covered by a pane of glass). The frescoes on the burial chamber walls depict various scenes, including the interment, and King Ay, Tutankhamun's successor, performing the ritual opening of the mouth before the mummified king.

LONGEST TOMB

The ★★ **Tomb of Ramesses VI** (No 9), one of the longest in the valley, has wall paintings illustrating several sections of the *Book of Gates*. The astronomical ceiling is quite remarkable: it shows a procession of the heavenly deities with solar boats, as well as the sky-goddess Nut devouring the sun at night and giving birth to it again in the morning. The entrance to the burial chamber is

Star Attractions
● Tomb of Tutankhamun
● Tomb of Ramesses VI

The Curse of Tutankhamun
Howard Carter dug for five seasons in vain, before discovering Tutankhamun's tomb on 4 November, 1922. He and his financial backer Lord Carnarvon entered the tomb secretly on the night before the official opening, and apparently stole several items from the more than 1700 precious objects buried inside. Lord Carnarvon died the following year from an infected mosquito bite, and this was the beginning of the myth of the Curse of Tutankhamun, as several deaths followed of people connected to the excavation.

In the tomb of Ramesses VI

Map on page 54

Tomb KV5

In 1995 a tomb was discovered by the American archaeologist Kent Weeks, and is now known as KV5. It is a complex of more than 100 rooms, believed to have been built as a mass grave for 50 of Ramesses II's more than 100 sons. So far only the remains of a few princes have been found. KV63 was found in 2006, but no mummies were inside.

A portrait of Ramesses III in his tomb

flanked by two enormous winged serpents. It seems that this tomb was meant for Ramesses V, and no one is certain why Ramesses VI is buried here.

DEEPEST AND LARGEST TOMBS

The **Tomb of Amenhotep II** (No 35) is one of the deepest in the valley, with over 90 steps inside. After it had been plundered it was used by priests to hide mummies from other despoiled graves. The 'wallpaper' was meant to resemble papyrus, the walls were coloured yellow and covered with hieroglyphics representing almost every section of the *Book of the Dead*. The magnificent ceiling, with bright stars in a dark-blue firmament, is reminiscent of naive painting. The main corridor comes to an end just before a trapdoor and pit; the burial chamber is on the right. The columns inside depict the pharaoh presenting offerings for Osiris, Anubis and Hathor. This is where the sarcophagus containing the pharaoh's mummy was discovered.

The ★★★ **Tomb of Seti I**, the most important and largest grave in the valley with masterfully executed reliefs, is closed for restoration.

The huge ★★★ **Tomb of Ramesses III**, cut out of the rock, shows clearly how all installations from the Amarnah era onwards adopted an almost straight ground-plan to allow life-giving rays of sunshine to penetrate into the sarcophagus chamber. Small side chambers in the front section of the corridor were decorated with pictures of craftsmen, store-rooms, ships and an image of paradise (4th chamber on the right) – unusual sights in royal tombs. The last niche on the left shows a harpist playing for the king, which gave the burial place its nickname, 'the harpist's tomb'.

QUEEN HATSHEPSUT

A path, rather steep in places, leads across the mountains from the Valley of the King to the ★★★ **Mortuary Temple of Hatshepsut** ❷ in the area known as the Deir al-Bahari (the temple is also accessible by road). Queen Hatshepsut still poses quite a few problems for Egyptologists. After the death of her father Tuthmosis I, she married her half-brother Tuthmosis II in order to secure power. He died young, however, and his only successor was Tuthmosis III, the son of a concubine. Tuthmosis III was too young to reign, and so Hatshepsut did so in his place, leaving pictorial proof of her claim to the throne and of her divinity.

The theory goes that Hatshepsut was murdered by Tuthmosis III once he had come of age in around 1468BC. The first thing he did on acceding to the throne was to replace the name of his stepmother with his own on all the temples and monuments he could find; according to the belief of the time, this meant that he extinguished the queen in the afterworld. Hatshepsut's mummy has never been found.

STRIKING MONUMENT

The mortuary temple at the foot of the 300-m (984-ft) high rock face was built by Queen Hatshepsut's chief of works, Senmut. The location of the temple and the ramps that connect the terraces make this one of the most striking monuments in Egypt. The middle terrace has a magnificent series of reliefs depicting Queen Hatshepsut's journey (she is always depicted as a man) to the

Star Attractions
● **Tomb of Seti I**
● **Tomb of Ramesses III**
● **Temple of Hatshepsut**

Below: bust of Hathor at the Temple of Hatshepsut (bottom)

Map on page 54

Map on page 54

Everyday images
The great advantage of the Tombs of the Nobles over the royal tombs is that the paintings they contain depict everyday life in ancient Egypt rather than life beyond the grave. The motifs include funeral banquets with musicians and dancers, farmers working in the fields, craftsmen and court scenes. The pattern hardly changes, however: the left-hand wall provides biographical information about the deceased, and the right-hand one depicts the funeral ceremony.

An exquisite relief from the wall of a tomb

land of Punt – possibly today's Somalia – in search of incense and myrrh; her reception by the fat queen of Punt; and the exchange and transport of goods. The second ramp leads to the upper halls. Reliefs here were demolished by Coptic monks when the temple served as a monastery.

It is interesting to note that the axis of the Mortuary Temple of Hatshepsut and of the Temple of Karnak on the opposite side of the Nile are in exact alignment with each other.

It was close to Hatshepsut's temple in 1881 that Egyptology experienced one of its finest hours. A cache of royal mummies discovered by local farmers yielded most of the kings of the 17th to 20th Dynasties, including Tuthmosis III, Seti I and Ramesses II and III.

TOMBS OF THE NOBLES

More than 500 graves of officials, high priests and nobles of the 11th to the 16th Dynasties have so far been discovered, and are referred to collectively as the ★★★ **Tombs of the Nobles ❸**. The finest lie near Sheikh Abd al-Qurnah, and the following in particular should be visited:

★★★ **The Tomb-Chapel of Nakht** (No 52), the royal astronomer of Tuthmosis IV. The picture of the funeral banquet shows three lightly clad women entertaining guests with music on flute, harp and lute. The relaxed air of the banquet provides entertainment for the deceased and protection against evil spirits.

★★★ **The Tomb of Rekhmire** (No 100), the richly decorated tomb of a vizier under Tuthmosis III, shows clearly his daily activities, from collecting tributes in foreign lands, including giraffes, elephants and Cretan vases, to collecting taxes in the homeland. The funeral procession looks very much like a funeral procession today in villages in Upper Egypt.

★★★ **The Tomb-Chapel of Ramose** (No 55), governor of Thebes and vizier under Amenhotep III and Akhenaten. He was one of the first supporters of the Aten cult, and moved to the new capital of Tell al-Amarnah *(see page 53)*. His tomb-chapel thus remained incomplete and has two distinct styles. Some of the reliefs date from before the Aten period, others were added during the time of Aten worship. The realistic depictions of the so-called Amarnah style contrast sharply with the idealised pre-Aten painting. This is noticeable on the rear wall of the burial chamber, where there is a traditional depiction of Amenhotep III with Ramose on the left, and the same scene rendered far more realistically on the right.

★★★ **The Tomb-Chapel of Menna** (No 69) was never actually meant for Menna, a scribe under Tuthmosis I. The pictures illustrating his life show him supervising the harvest, measuring and calculating, while nearby young girls play and pull each other's hair and a young boy plays the flute – a real rural idyll.

★★ **The Tomb-Chapel of Sennufer** (No 96) is also known as the Tomb of the Vine because of its plant paintings on the ceiling; it's like being in the middle of a vineyard. Sennufer was the mayor of Thebes during the reign of Amenhotep II, and probably the chief vintner, too.

COLOSSI OF RAMESSES

★ **The Ramesseum** ❹ was erected as a mortuary temple by Ramesses II for himself and Amun.

Star Attraction
● Tombs of the Nobles

Below: Anubis anointing the dead
Bottom: the paintings from the tombs give clues to more than mortuary rites

Map
on page
54

*Below: a village near the
Valley of the Kings
Bottom: the Ramesseum*

Had the temple remained intact it would probably have surpassed the grandeur of Ramesses II's temple at Abu Simbel, but it was built on land that was annually inundated and it soon collapsed. The toppled colossi of Ramesses II, a symbol of his vanity and self-glorification, which inspired Shelley's famous sonnet of *Ozymandias*, are the temple's main sight. The carvings are familiar to those who have already visited Karnak: scenes from the Battle of Kadesh and the wars against the Hittites, showing Ramesses II as a soldier.

BEST PRESERVED TEMPLE

The ★ ★ ★ **Mortuary Temple of Ramesses III** ❺ at Madinat Habu is a clear copy of the Ramesseum. Ramesses III's 20th-Dynasty temple is the last of the classical temples and one of the best preserved in Egypt. The enclosure is entered through an unusual gatehouse containing the private pleasure apartments of the pharaoh. The reliefs, also copied from Ramesses II's temple, show Ramesses III in battles he never fought. The first Court shows glorious carvings, some still coloured, of festivities and ceremonies, and through a window the ruins of the royal palace. Three small hypostyle halls lead to the inner sanctuaries. Walk around the outer walls to admire scenes of Ramesses III hunting and fishing.

VALLEY OF THE QUEENS

So far, 70 tombs have been discovered in the ★★★ **Valley of the Queens ❻**. They resemble those of the Valley of the Kings in design, although they are somewhat smaller, and their existence is interpreted as a mark of respect on the part of the pharaohs for their wives and mothers, whose political influence was often considerable.

The most magnificent tomb is the completely restored ★★★ **Tomb of Queen Nefertari**, beloved wife of Ramesses II. It is the only one that was completely decorated: it contains pictures from the *Book of the Dead* and portraits of the pretty queen seated in front of Osiris, with Isis, or alone in front of a pavilion playing a game resembling chess. The starry firmament in the burial chamber is exceptionally fine. Only a limited number of tickets to the site are sold every day.

The ★★ **Tomb-Chapel of Prince Amun hir Khopshef** is notable for the freshness of its colours, especially the blue. Ramesses III built this tomb for his son, who died young. There is something touching about the pictures of the over-sized father accompanying his son (the plaited hair symbolises youth) to the afterworld and introducing him to the gods Thoth, Ptah and Isis.

The ★★ **Tomb of Prince Kha'emweset** shows another son of Ramesses III being introduced to the deities of the afterworld. The reliefs showing the prince making offerings to the gods are among the best preserved of their time (20th dynasty), although Ramesses III seems to be depicted here rather more often than his son.

GREEK HERO

On the way back to the Nile ferry, don't forget to stop briefly to admire the enormous sandstone **Colossi of Memnon ❼**, formerly part of the royal mortuary temple of Amenhotep III. These two huge seated figures are 19m (62ft) high, and covered with ancient graffiti scratched by, among others, the Emperor Hadrian and other travellers of antiquity. The Greeks thought the statues represented the Trojan hero Memnon, son of the goddess

Deir al-Medinah

The workmen and artisans who worked on the tombs of the pharaohs lived in Deir al-Medinah, opposite today's ticket office. As they recorded their daily life on papyrus and pottery, we know that they worked shifts of eight hours for ten days. In their time off they worked on their own tombs, often inspired by the royal tombs. A few tombs, particularly of Sennedjem, Peshedu and Inherkhau, are worth visiting for the beautiful wall decorations.

A Colossus of Memnon

Map
on page
54

The New Year festival
On the eve of the ancient New Year, at the end of the inundation season, when the waters of the Nile receded, an important festival took place. The statues of Hathor and other gods were taken to the roof of the temple, where they united with the sun, who gave power and strength for the coming growing season. The procession is illustrated on the walls of the staircase leading to the roof of the temple in Dendera.

Eos, who was killed by Achilles – hence the name.

The valley here has several other mortuary temples all in a more or less ruinous state. The best of these temples was built by Seti I, near Howard Carter's house in **Al-Qurnah**. The monuments from the reign of Seti I are among the finest of the New Kingdom period. He built this temple in honour of his father Ramesses I and the god Amun, but very little of it remains. Having said that, the temple is rarely visited, and you are likely to find yourself on your own to view the superb carvings on the columns and the sanctuary walls.

EXCURSIONS

Luxor is the ideal starting point for excursions into Upper Egypt, but before venturing north to Dendera and Abydos you are strongly advised to check whether any safety warnings against travel are currently in force. In recent years this area, and up to Asyut *(see page 53)*, have witnessed acts of Islamic terrorism, and travel can only be done twice a day in armed convoy (check with the tourist office for timetables and arrangements before you travel).

Located 67km (42 miles) to the north on the western bank of the Nile is the ★★★ **Temple of Dendera**, dedicated to the sky and fertility goddess Hathor. She was worshipped here along with her husband Horus and son Ihy, the god of music. The Temple of Dendera was built during the Graeco-Roman period (125BC – AD60) by three Roman emperors: Domitian, Nerva and Trajan.

The temple is one of the best-preserved of this period. It is enclosed by a mudbrick wall and entered by a Roman gateway. There is a particularly fine relief on the outer wall showing Cleopatra with Caesarion, the son she had by Gaius Julius Caesar. The hypostyle hall has 24 Hathoric columns and a ceiling decorated with colourful scenes from the Egyptian zodiac. A staircase leads to the roof and the Disc Chapel, where the statue of Hathor resided for the New Year festival *(see box)*. Also on the roof are the Chapels of Osiris, with a plaster cast of the famous Dendera zodiac. The original is in the Louvre in Paris.

A local man in Luxor

SACRED TOWN

Near the town of Al-Balyana, 98km (61 miles) to the north of Dendera and 165km (102 miles) north of Luxor, is the site of ★★ **Abydos**. During the 5th dynasty this was the site of Egypt's central necropolis, protected by the dog-headed god Chontamenti. When the death cult granted ordinary people resurrection in the afterworld, and not only kings, every mummy took a ritual trip here.

As well as being considered the entrance to the afterworld, the temple later became associated with the legend of Osiris. In this, Osiris is killed by his brother Seth, and brought back to life by his wife Isis *(see pages 71–2)*. Osiris's dismembered body was buried across the country. His head was buried at Abydos, where he was resurrected as king of the afterworld.

Abydos contains one of the most magnificent temples in Egypt, the ★★★**Great Temple of Seti I**, completed by Ramesses II for his late father. The reliefs are well-preserved, and their motifs are repeated in other Ramessid temples: the fight against the Hittites, and Ramesses II among the gods. The real highlight is the **Abydos List of Kings** at the left exit from the second hypostyle hall. Seti, with the young Ramesses before him, honours his 76 predecessors. The list was invaluable to Egyptologists as a source for the chronology of the dynasties.

Star Attractions
● Temple of Dendera
● Abydos
● Great Temple of Seti I

Below: Islamic prayers at the Temple of Dendera
Bottom: Temple of Seti I

6: Luxor to Aswan

Many tourists visiting Egypt take a cruise on the Nile from Luxor to Aswan or the other way around. A more idyllic, albeit not very luxurious, way is to sail the route as the ancients must have done in a *felucca*, which takes four days, wind willing. It is also possible to do the route overland, but at the time of writing the only way to visit the temples by car or bus is to travel in armed convoy, which leaves twice a day. Check with the tourist offices in Aswan or Luxor for the current situation.

The Corniche road from Luxor goes south along the Nile. Just before arriving at Esna are two barrages, one built in 1906 by the British and one in the 1990s, known as the 'Electricity Bridge'. If the water is not high enough, tourists on cruise boats may have to change boats here. In the peak season there are queues to pass through the lock.

Map below

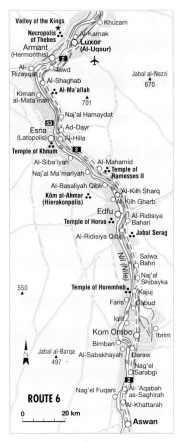

Valley of the Kings
Khuzam
Necropolis of Thebes
Al-Karnak
Armant (Hermonthis)
Luxor (Al-Uqsur)
Al-Rizayqat
Tawd
Jabal al-Nezzi 670
Al-Shaghab
Al-Ma'allah 701
Kiman al-Mata'inah
Naj'al Hamaydat
Esna (Latopolis)
Ad-Dayr
Al-Hilla
Temple of Khnum
Al-Siba'iyah
Al-Mahamid
Naj'al Ma'mariyah
Temple of Ramesses II
Al-Basaliyah Qibli
Kôm al-Ahmar (Hierakonpolis)
Al-Kilh Sharq
Al-Kilh Gharb
Edfu
Al-Ridisiya Bahari
Temple of Horus
Al-Ridisiya Qibli
Jabal Serag
Salwa Bahri
Naj'al Shibayka
Temple of Horemheb
Kajuj
550
Faris
Dabud
Iqlit
Kom Ombo
Ibrim
Bimban
Jabal al-Barqa 497
Al-Sabakhayah
Daraw
Nag'el Sarabgi
Nag'el Fuqani
Al-'Aqabah as-Saghirah
Al-Khattarah
ROUTE 6
Aswan
0   20 km
N

CARAVAN TERMINAL

The small provincial town of **Esna** is 53km (33 miles) south of Luxor. Nowadays it is hard to imagine that Esna was one of the most important places in Upper Egypt – it used to be the Nile terminal for the Sudan caravan routes. It is also no longer the exotic place where the French writer Gustave Flaubert hung out in brothels and watched provocative belly dancing. The only reason for visiting Esna is for the remains of its temple, a short walk through the souk from the Nile. The ★★**Temple of Khnum** (open daily 6am–5pm in summer, 4pm in winter), the ram-headed god, was built around 181BC by Ptolemy VI. At the time it was probably as large as the temple at Edfu, but most of the temple is now hidden beneath the houses. Only the hypostyle hall, added in the 1st century AD by the Roman emperor Claudius, was excavated in 1860. It is approached by a staircase as the temple now lies 10m (33ft) below street level. The roof is supported by

24 fine columns with different floral capitals, representing a real garden. The astronomical ceiling has almost disappeared as it was used as a church by the early Christians. The wall carvings depict the Roman emperors Claudius, Vespasian, Trajan and Hadrian dressed as pharaohs and making offerings to the Egyptian gods.

OSIRIS MYTH

Half way between Luxor and Aswan, about 64 km (40 miles) from Esna, lies **Edfu**, on the site of the ancient city of **Djeba**, where Horus with the Winged Disk was worshipped. Edfu is also closely connected with the Osiris myth. When the god Osiris became king and married his sister Isis, life in Egypt was sweet and rosy. Overcome with jealousy, his brother Seth trapped Osiris in a coffin and dropped him in the Nile. The coffin floated down to the Mediterranean and up to the coast near Byblos (now in Lebanon). Isis eventually found her husband's body and brought it back to Egypt. Seth cut the corpse in 14 pieces, which he again threw in the Nile. Isis found 13 pieces but the penis had been eaten by a fish. Isis reassembled the body, took it to Abydos, made a phallus out of clay and wrapped him in bandages, so he became the first mummy. Many reliefs in temples all over Egypt show Isis as a

Star Attraction
● Temple of Khuum

The Forty Days Road
Camels come from Darfur in the Sudan and are walked along an ancient caravan trail for 40 days through the Libyan Desert to Dongola. From there they follow the Nile into Egypt. The Sudanese camel drovers belong to two particular tribes and are instantly recognisable from their traditional gear. Camels at Daraw are cheaper than in the Cairo camel market of Birqash.

A statue of Horus at Edfu

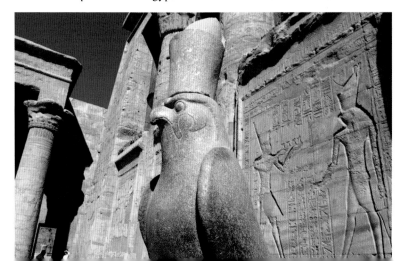

Map on page 70

Twin temples
The Temple of Hathor in Dendera was modelled on the Temple of Edfu, as the two are intimately connected, like the temples of Luxor and Karnak. Once a year amidst huge fertility celebrations Horus was reunited with his wife Hathor at the temple of Dendera.

bird hovering over the erect phallus. Isis was able to revive Osiris long enough for their son Horus to be conceived. When Horus became a man, he avenged his father, killing his uncle Seth at Edfu.

The ★★★**Temple of Horus** (open daily 6am–5pm in summer; 6am–4pm in winter) was built by the Ptolemies between 257 and 237BC in the classic pharaonic style. It is the best-preserved temple complex in Egypt, as it was completely covered with sand until the 1860s when Auguste Mariette started excavating it. The visit should start at the massive pylon (gateway) built by Ptolemy IX. The inside walls record the Festival of the Beautiful Meeting, when Horus joined Hathor in Dendera (see page 68).

The first hypostyle hall is guarded by some magnificent hawk statues, and the inside walls show the foundation rituals of the temple, with the pharaoh putting down the mud-bricks. The sanctuary once contained the sacred barge of Horus. The New Year chapel reveals a fine depiction of the sky goddess Nut, and a relief of Horus' victory over Seth depicted as a hippo.

NUBIAN TOWN

Hieroglyphs retaining their original colours at Kom Ombo

Further south along the Nile (56 km/35 miles) is the town of **Kom Ombo**, where many Nubian families displaced by the building of the Aswan High Dam were resettled. Like Esna, Kom Ombo was an important trading post in ancient times, as it stood on the crossroads of the caravan trail from Nubia to the gold mines in the Eastern Desert. The setting of the temple in Kom Ombo is one of the most picturesque in Egypt, on a low promontory in a bend of the river, although part of the temple complex has disappeared into the Nile. The ★★**Temple of Kom Ombo** (open daily 7am–5pm in summer, 7am–4pm in winter) is unusually dedicated to two gods: the right side is dedicated to the crocodile god Sobek, the left side to Horus the Elder or Haruris, known as the Good Doctor. The two sides are symmetrical.

Ptolemy VI started building the temple around 180BC, but most of the building was done under

Neos Dionysos (80–51BC) and the Roman Emperor Augustus (30BC–AD14). The First Pylon, forecourt and birth house have mostly disappeared in the Nile, and the 1992 earthquake afflicted serious damage, but there is still plenty worth visiting. To the right of the massive gateway is a small chapel of Hathor, which contains crocodile mummies found nearby. The First Hypostyle Hall has two gates leading into the twin sanctuaries. The left part of the facade shows Neos Dionysos in front of Horus, while on the right he appears in front of Sobek. The ceiling of the Hall, supported by superb floral columns, is decorated with flying vultures. The walls of the older Second Hypostyle Hall depict Ptolemy VI making offerings to the gods. On the door between the twin sanctuaries is a superb depiction of Ptolemy VI and his wife receiving a palm branch. At the back of the sanctuaries are the Carving of the Ear Chapels, where pilgrims put their petitions to the gods. Many came here in the hope of a cure for their ailments.

CAMEL MARKET

Around 5 km (3 miles) further south is **Daraw**, where an important camel market takes place daily (6.30am–2pm), though the principle market day is Sunday. Watch out for loose-running camels. Aswan is 40 km (25 miles) away.

Star Attractions
● **Temple of Horus**
● **Temple of Kom Ombo**

Below: the Hypostyle Hall, Kom Ombo
Bottom: at the Daraw camel market

7: Aswan

Map below

Aswan lies on the northern border of Nubia and was once one of the most important towns in Egypt. It was popular with the British as a winter resort during colonial times, and it was here that Agatha Christie wrote her best-selling novel *Death on the Nile*. The third Aga Khan was well acquainted with the beauty of Aswan where he spent the winter months, and asked in his will to be buried here – his wish was duly carried out.

Many of the 245,000 population are Nubians, who are among the friendliest people in Egypt. The bazaar traders, taxi drivers and coachmen are far less pushy and insistent than their counterparts in, say, Luxor. Aswan truly feels like the gateway to Africa.

Construction of the nearby Aswan High Dam brought unexpected climatic changes in its wake. It has altered the pattern of rainfall and the humidity can be tropical in its intensity. In the summer Aswan is almost unbearably hot, with afternoon temperatures often as high as 45°C (113°F).

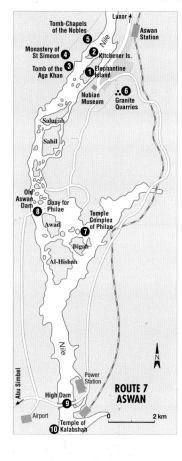

HISTORY

Swen was the ancient Egyptian name for Aswan. For the pharaohs, Aswan wasn't merely the place where granite was quarried for their temples; it was also the end of the world – the source of the Nile was assumed to be just beyond the First Cataract. During the Old Kingdom a few travellers ventured further up the Nile in quest of gold, slaves and the occasional pygmy. By the time the Greeks called it *Syene*, Aswan was an important caravan centre, ivory market and control post for trade with Nubia and Central Africa.

SIGHTS

Ferries link the Corniche with **Elephantine Island ❶**. On the island are the ruins of the ancient city of Yebu (the name means 'elephant' and points to the island's importance for the ivory trade). The main sight on the island is the small **Aswan Museum** (open daily 8am–4pm, 5pm in summer). The most interesting items were moved to the Nubian museum *(see page 77)*, but a few exhibits from the island's **Temple of Satet** are worth a look, and the garden offers a welcome shady refuge. The ticket also permits entrance to the ruins of **Yebu** and to the **Nilometer**. This was the first Nilometer to measure the river's rise, from which the priests calculated the rate of taxation. It was constructed during Roman times, on the site of an earlier one, and reveals marks in Arabic, Roman and pharaonic numerals.

Further south, research and restoration work by a German and Swiss archaeological team enabled the reconstruction of the temple devoted to **Satet**, the bringer of the Nile floods, which was once located here. Close by are the ruins of a temple to the ram-headed god Khnum, surrounded by the former living quarters of the priests and officials.

To the north of the island are two Nubian villages with lush gardens which make for an interesting stroll.

ISLAND TOUR

Feluccas – small sailing boats – cross to **Kitchener Island ❷**, formerly the property of the

> ### The First Cataract
> The ancient Egyptians believed that the First Cataract was the source of the Nile, from where the river went south into the Sudan, and north into Egypt. It was where the gods Khnum or Hapi lived who controlled the flood of the Nile. Until the building of the Aswan Dam, the boiling and twirling waters of the cataract were a serious obstacle for upstream travel. Today the 4km (2mile) journey upriver provides a pleasant and quieter alternative to the usual *felucca* ride around the islands, combined with a visit to Sahil Island.

Elephantine Island

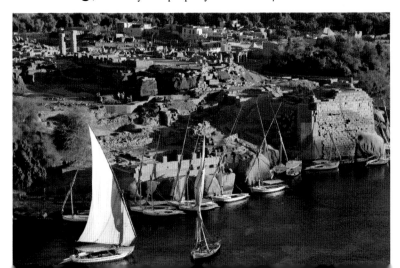

Map on page 74

Below: looking across to the Aga Khan mausoleum
Bottom: Temple Complex of Philae

military British proconsul Horatio Herbert Kitchener, who ruled Egypt and the Sudan from 1911 to 1914. After a walk through the botanical gardens, take a boat across to the west bank opposite the south tip of Elephantine Island and go to the **Tomb of the Aga Khan ❸** (closed to the public) for magnificent views over the river. The third Aga Khan, leader of the Shiite sect of Ismaili Muslims, died in 1957, and his burial on 20 February 1959 was an international event.

The nearby **Monastery of St Simeon ❹** was founded in the 7th century, but the present structure dates from the 10th century (an earlier one on the site was destroyed by Saladin). The compound is on two levels, and enclosed by a 6m (20ft) high wall. The lower enclosure is a basilica; a flight of steps from inside the church leads to the upper enclosure, with kitchen, refectory and sleeping quarters. The monastery was deserted in the 13th century due to water shortage.

PRINCES' TOMBS

The best way to reach the ★ **Tomb-Chapels of the Nobles ❺** is by *felucca*. Local princes and nobles from the Old Kingdom are buried here.

One tomb in particular merits closer inspection, that of **Sirenput II**, a prince of the 12th Dynasty. The best paintings can be found in the burial

chamber. They show Sirenput sitting at a table with his son and his mother, and his wife looking after the three of them.

NUBIAN CULTURE

The ★★★**Nubian Museum** (open 9am–1pm and 5–10pm, summer 6–10pm), one of the finest in Egypt, is dedicated to Nubian culture from prehistoric times to the modern era before the construction of the Aswan Dam.

One part of the museum has a rich collection of artefacts from Nubian historic sights, often revealing the particular style of the region. The other half is dedicated to Nubian folklore and traditions. More sculpture is on show in the surrounding garden, as well as Islamic shrines and prehistoric wall carvings of animals.

One particularly fascinating excursion from Aswan is to the **Granite Quarries ❻**. Whole armies of people toiled here during antiquity, cutting huge blocks of pink granite from the rock face. The unfinished obelisk gives an idea of just how hard they worked: it is 42m (137ft) long and weighs an estimated 1,168 tons.

SUBMERGED TEMPLE

To reach the ★★★ **Temple Complex of Philae ❼** (open daily 7am–5pm in summer, 7am–4pm in winter), turn left to the ferry docks before the old dam and travel across by motor boat. Philae was submerged for nine months of every year after the old Aswan Dam was built, and the construction of the High Dam would have placed it completely under water had it not been rescued. All the structures, comprising 40,000 stone blocks, were carefully shifted and then reassembled on the neighbouring island of Agiliqiyyah. The largest structure at Philae is the **Temple of Isis** (built around 350BC). The colonnade court at the front ends at the First Pylon of Ptolemy XII, with enormous reliefs of the king.

Behind the Second Pylon lies the hypostyle hall converted in the 6th century into a church, and the dark Sanctuary where a pedestal that once sup-

Star Attractions
● Nubian Museum
● Temple Complex of Philae

The Nubian diaspora
The building of the High Dam created the vast Lake Nasser, which flooded parts of Nubia. The most important monuments were salvaged by the international community, but the Nubians lost their lands, their culture and a lot of their traditions. A few moved to Aswan or the villages around it, but most of the 800,000-strong displaced community moved on to Cairo, to Sudan or abroad. Nubians have done remarkably well for themselves, and many enjoyed higher education. The Nubian Museum is the first project to honour their long history and culture.

The Nile and Philae

Map on page 74

ported Isis's sacred barque is still in place. To the right of the Temple of Isis is the Kiosk of Trajan, with beautifully carved columns, and the Temple of Hathor with a fine relief of musicians. A *son et lumière* show takes place here twice a day.

THE ASWAN DAMS

Despite its height of 51m (167ft), the **Old Aswan Dam** (1898–1902) ❽ was inadequate against the annual Nile flood, but it did guarantee Egypt's survival, because the waters of its reservoir added 16 percent more arable land to the country.

The construction of a new dam was inevitable. The gigantic **High Dam** ❾ was built, with Soviet help, between 1960 and 1971: it is 111m (364ft) high, 3½km (2 miles) long, 1km (⅔ mile) wide, and the reservoir behind it, **Lake Nasser**, extends about 500km (310 miles). Since the dam's construction there have been no more floods and the harvest yield has increased by 20 percent.

The **★★ Temple of Kalabshah** ❿ (open daily 8am–4pm) was moved 38km (23 miles) north of its original site to make way for the reservoir of the new High Dam. The relocation work was carried out by a team of West German engineers, and completed in 1975. The temple was consecrated to the Nubian god Mandulis, the equivalent of the pharaonic god Horus. The cult of Isis was equally important: each year the image of the goddess Isis was taken from Philae to Kalabshah. Much of the temple was completed during the reign of the Roman emperor Augustus.

ABU SIMBEL

★★★ Abu Simbel (open daily 6am–6pm in summer; 6am–5pm in winter), the site of two temples built by Ramesses II, can be reached by air several times a day from Cairo, Luxor and Aswan, as well as by bus and taxi in convoys from Aswan.

Abu Simbel was dedicated to the gods Amun, Horakhte and Ptah. Its sheer size was meant to demonstrate the might of Egypt and frighten away would-be invaders. The 31-m (102-ft) high facade

👁 **Cruises on Lake Nasser**
Those who find the Nile overcrowded with cruise boats can enjoy the peace and quiet of a cruise on Lake Nasser, from Aswan to Abu Simbel or vice versa. The cruise takes in the Kalabshah Temple, and the isolated Nubian temples of Qasr Ibrim, Amada, Dayr, Mehrarakka, Wadi es-Seboua and Dakka, which can only be reached by boat. The stylish M/S Eugénie, Kasr Ibrim and Prince Abbas cruise ships make 3, 4 or 7 day cruises (tel: 02-2516 9653) but similar cruises are also offered on three other luxurious vessels which can be booked at any travel agent.

Feluccas *near Aswan*

of the ★★★**Great Sun Temple** is world-famous: its four **colossal statues**, each 20m (65ft) high, represent the Pharaoh Ramesses II enthroned. The statues stare eastwards towards the rising sun. Each of the colossi wears the royal double crown and headcloth. Carved around their feet are small figures representing Ramesses' queen, Nefertari, and several of his children (he had over 200).

Star Attractions
● **Temple of Kalabshah**
● **Abu Simbel**
● **Great Sun Temple**

SUN TRAP

The temple consists of three consecutive halls extending 56m (184ft) into the cliff, built in such a way that twice a year, on 21 February and 21 October, the first rays of the rising sun shone straight through the portal and all the way down the 65m (213ft) corridor inside the mountain, illuminating the shrine in the innermost sanctuary. The reliefs inside show Ramesses II fighting the Hittites at the Battle of Kadesh. Next to the Great Temple is a smaller one, dedicated to Ramesses' wife Nefertari for the worship of the goddess Hathor, and adorned with 10m (33ft) statues of the king and queen.

The entire temple complex was raised 64m (210ft) and re-positioned 180m (590ft) inland between 1965 and 1968. Following the relocation, the sun now shines into the temple one day later, on 22 February and 22 October.

Below and bottom: the Temple of Abu Simbel

Map on page 81

Map on page 81

Visiting hours

Visiting hours vary from monastery to monastery, and all monasteries, except for Deir Anba Bishoi, are closed during the many Coptic festivals. Deir Maqariyus is always closed, except for those who have a letter of introduction from the Coptic Patriarchate on 222, Sharia Ramesses in Cairo tel: (02) 2282 5374/2590 0218. They can also advise on opening times, and will write permission letters for male visitors only to stay at the monasteries.

8: The Pilgrim's Way

Cairo – Alexandria – Cairo

Cairo is connected to Alexandria by two roads, each of them around 220km (137 miles) long: one is a motorway through the desert and the other a main road, through the fertile delta of the Nile. These routes are popular with pilgrims. Christians head for the desert monasteries in the Wadi Natrun, and once a year Sufi Muslims travel to Tanta to celebrate the *mawlid* (festival) of the Islamic mystic, Sayed Ahmed al-Badawi.

ROUND TRIP

If you make this a round trip it will take two days, not including time for seeing the sights of Alexandria. Leave Cairo, passing the Pyramids, and travel 90km (56 miles) along the desert road as far as the service area. Follow signs off to the right to the **Wadi Natrun**, a popular Coptic place of pilgrimage. The word *wadi* means valley, and Natrun is an indicator of the many dried-up lakes here in the summer which leave deposits of salt and natron (hydrous sodium carbonate). Natron was used by ancient Egyptians in mummification to dehydrate the corpse, and later by the Romans in glass-making.

Christianity arrived in Egypt via Alexandria, and this region has been Christian since the 4th century. The early settlers founded around 100 hermitage monasteries at the Wadi Natrun. The holy family is believed to have stayed close to the four great monasteries that survive.

PATRIARCHS' ROOTS

The wadi is 32km (20 miles) long, and 10,000 people live here. Several new buildings have appeared next to these fortress-like monasteries in recent years; monasticism is still very popular in Egypt, and the Wadi Natrun supplies many patriarchs for the Coptic Church. The monasteries are closed during major Coptic festivals, but at other times the monks are happy to provide guided tours. The

Deir Anba Bishoi

easiest accessible is the **Deir Anba Bishoi** (founded in AD390), one of the earliest monasteries in Wadi Natrun, with five churches. The multi-domed building is the residence of the current Egyptian Pope, Baba Shenouda III.

The monastery of ★ **Deir al-Suryani** ('the monastery of the Syrians') comes into view soon after. The basilica contains a central chapel consecrated to the Virgin that is a magnificent example of Coptic religious art.

★★ **Deir Maqariyus** lies in the southwestern part of the wadi, and is the best-preserved monastery in Egypt. It was founded by St Macarius the Great (AD300–390), a cameleer who, after visiting St Antony, the founder of monasticism, retired to the wadi and built the monastery. It was destroyed several times before the patriarch Shenouda rebuilt it in its present form in the 9th century. Most Coptic popes were chosen from this monastery.

Deir al-Baramus, Coptic for 'Two Romans', is the oldest and most isolated of the monasteries. The St John's Church has a wonderful

Star Attraction
● **Deir Maqariyus monastery**

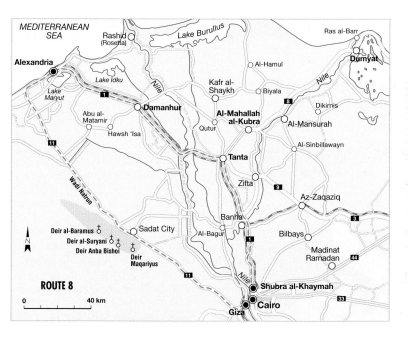

Map on page 81

iconostasis inlaid with ivory. Meanwhile, restorations in the 9th-century al-Adhra Church revealed medieval frescoes.

THE NILE DELTA

Alexandria *(see page 45)* is around 121km (75 miles) drive along the desert motorway. Before reaching the city, the route leads along an embankment across **Lake Maryut**, a shallow basin where reeds flourish.

Leave Alexandria from the southeast. The view from the road across the Nile Delta is typical of rural Egypt, and the rapid succession of villages along the route underlines the density of Egypt's population. The road is lined with fields of cotton, wheat, fruit and vegetables; *fellahin* (farm workers) can be seen ploughing their fields with oxen and pumping water with wooden waterwheels. Control of the Nile floods by dams has meant that three harvests a year are now possible. Women wash clothes in the dark green canal water, and horses and donkeys are watered here, too. Be careful not to touch the water, however: there's a risk of being infected with bilharzia (an infestation of tiny worms).

A Jewish *mouled*

Egypt's only Jewish *mouled* is held near the shrine of Abu Khatzeira ('Father of the Mat') in Damanhur over two days in January. Abu Khatzeira was a 19th-century mystic who lived in Damanhur. In recent years the fear of terrorism has meant heavy security, but a few thousand mainly Israeli and French pilgrims still come to the festival.

In the Nile Delta

COTTON TOWN

Drive in the direction of Tanta now. **Damanhur** (pop. 320,000; 65km/40 miles) is the centre of Egypt's cotton industry. Once the international market leader, the industry has been in recession since 1994. The busy town's *souk* is worth a visit.

Continue for another 65km (40 miles) to the university town of **Tanta**, which is the main traffic junction of the Nile Delta. The annual *mawlid* celebrations are held here in honour of the mystic Sayed Ahmed al-Badawi, who died in the town in 1273. The charismatic Badawi was a legend even during his lifetime. Disciples came to his funeral from as far away as India. Hundreds of thousands of pilgrims celebrate the famous miracle-worker with a week-long fair, involving snake-charmers, horse ballets and dervishes.

From Tanta, it's 100km (62 miles) back to Cairo.

9: Port Said to Hurghadah

Port Said – Al-Isma'iliyyah – Suez – Hurghadah

Oil refineries, the Suez Canal, the Port Said free trade zone…This route runs through Egypt's modern industrial region, and the trip can be done equally well by taxi, car or bus. The Suez Canal tolls alone bring in around US\$2 billion annually. Even during antiquity there used to be a narrow channel connecting the Red Sea and the Mediterranean; today the Suez Canal is the most-travelled stretch of water in the world.

CANAL CITIES

Port Said and its sister city of Port Fuad were founded in 1859, during construction of the Suez Canal. The outer harbour was carefully designed so that its two protecting breakwaters would prevent coastal currents from silting up the canal. Opposite Port Said's white harbour building – a relic of the British occupation – is a magnificent mosque built in 1993. Port Said is a tax-free industrial zone. Its ★ **Military Museum** (open Sat–Thur 9am–3pm) features information on the Israeli wars as well as pharaonic and Islamic warfare, and is worth a visit.

From Port Said it is 80km (50 miles) to **Al-Isma'iliyyah**. If you take the train the railway line

Map on page 84

Below: Port Said waterfront
Bottom: the Suez Canal administrative buildings overlook the waterway

runs parallel to the Suez Canal, providing an excellent view of the enormous ships as they glide past.

The seat of the Suez Canal Authority, Al-Isma'iliyyah is one of the greenest towns in Egypt. It lies on the bank of **Lake Timsah** (the name means 'crocodile' but there aren't any left) and is a popular holiday resort for Egyptians.

SUEZ CANAL

The town of **Suez** is 91km (56 miles) south of Al-Isma'iliyyah. During the October War of 1973 with Israel almost 80 percent of the town was destroyed, but reconstruction work has been swift. The region now has a population of over 600,000. Suez itself has little of interest to offer, apart from having given its name to the ★★**Suez Canal**. Ferdinand de Lesseps, the French vice-consul in Egypt, succeeded in gaining permission to construct this world-famous waterway, which was opened in 1869 and is 160km (99 miles) long. It saved shipping from having to travel right round Africa, almost halving the journey time between Europe and the Far East.

ROUTE 9

WAR WITH ISRAEL

After the Suez Crisis of 1956 and the Six Day War of 1967, during which Egypt was dealt a crushing blow by the Israeli air force, President Anwar al-Sadat was keen to recapture the Sinai. He planned the attack for 6 October, 1973 – Yom Kippur, Israel's biggest religious holiday. Although the Israeli prime minister Golda Meir knew of the plan, she couldn't count on American support. The US wanted to win back political ground in the Middle East. In the event of an attack, Egypt and the US had already decided on a limited military victory with a subsequent solution of the conflict at the negotiating table.

After initial successes, the Egyptians soon lost the upper hand. When the Israelis finally closed the Suez–Cairo route on 21 October and threatened to encircle Egypt's army completely, things looked very gloomy for Sadat and he agreed to a cease-fire – after all, he could count on getting back the Sinai at the negotiating table. Thus, despite military defeat, he got what he wanted, and the US was also able to gain a foothold in the Middle East. This paved the way for the Camp David accords (1979) and subsequent peace negotiations.

MOUNTAIN RETREAT

South of Suez are several beach resorts popular with Cairenes, including **Ayn Sukhnah**. At Al-Za'faranah turn away from the coast, on to the road to Bani Suwayf. After just under 40km (25 miles) a left turn leads up to the ★★ **Monastery of St Anthony** (tel: 02-2590 0218; open daily 9am–5pm; closed during Lent and Christmas). St Anthony, the patron saint of prisoners, was born in AD251 in Upper Egypt. When he lost his parents at 18 he decided to become a hermit in search of a purer experience of Christianity. His followers drove him ever further into the wilderness, until he ended up in the cave in **Mount Qalah** where he remained for the rest of his life until he died at the age of 105. The monastery was founded after St Anthony's death. In the following

Star Attractions
● **Suez Canal**
● **Monastery of St Anthony**

The Suez Canal
Fourteen percent of world trade travels through this canal, and from the very start this economically and strategically important waterway has been the focus of attention of the world's major powers, especially the British and the French. In 1956 it was nationalised by President Nasser, sparking off the notorious Suez Crisis; in 1967 Israel occupied the Sinai as far as the canal.

Morning prayers at St Anthony's

Map
on page
84

Map on page 84

Red Sea monasteries
The two monasteries of St Anthony and St Paul are the object of pilgrimage for thousands of Egyptian Christians on certain feast days during the year. For the rest of the year the monks lead a quiet life of work and prayer, very much as they did 15 centuries ago when the original Desert Fathers retired from the fever and injustice of the world to seek a better way of life.

centuries it was often raided by Bedouin, but in the 12th century it was restored by the Coptic monks. Now some 60 Coptic monks live and work in the monastery, one of whom will give a tour of the compound, including the churches, the keep, the kitchen and the library. The oldest church, dedicated to St Anthony, has some fine 13th-century murals.

St Anthony's Cave is a 2km (1 mile) walk from the monastery and it involves 1,200 steps. Age-old graffiti and more recent scraps of paper have been left by the many pilgrims who have visited the cave. The views over the wadis below and the Red Sea are magnificent.

THE FIRST HERMIT

Return to Al-Za'faranah and continue south along the coastal road for 26km (16 miles) for the turn-off for ★★**St Paul's Monastery** (open daily 9am–5pm; closed during Lent and Christmas). Set in a rocky desert landscape and surrounded by high walls, it was consecrated to St Paul the Theban. To escape the persecutions of the Emperor Decius, 16-year-old St Paul fled from Alexandria to the Red Mountains to become the earliest known hermit. He lived in a cave for more than 80 years, and just before his death he was visited by St Anthony. It was St Anthony who buried him with the help of two lions.

The monastery was built by St Paul's followers around his cave. It is much smaller and more simple than St Anthony's. The monks will show you the tiny Church of St Paul, the keep where they used to hide from attacking Bedouin, and the Church of St Michael.

WEALTHY PLAYGROUND

Back on the main coastal road, the route leads southwards past many holiday resorts. After about 275km (171 miles) the road passes the resort town of **Al-Gouna**, created in the 1990s. The resort is built around several lagoons and, apart from some pleasant hotels, it has a large amount of hol-

Mosaic at St Anthony's

iday homes mostly owned by Cairenes. Al-Gouna has become the playground of many wealthy young Cairenes who congregate here on weekends and during the holidays. It has a large shopping centre, a golf course, an open-air cinema, nightclubs, bars, a hospital and a casino.

Below: a fully clothed swim at Hurghadah
Bottom: Hurghadah's spectacular backdrop

Wealthy Playground

A further 25km (16 miles) to the south is ★★**Hurghadah**, formerly a small fishing village with some huts belonging to British oil prospectors. Today it is the favourite destination for travellers who want to combine a tour of the antiquities with a stay at the seaside.

The sun shines 350 days a year, the desert mountains provide a magnificent backdrop, the wind blows off the land (making it ideal for windsurfing and sailing), and the waters are perfect for diving and snorkelling.

Over 25km (16 miles) of hotels and bungalow villages now stretch along the coast. This may seem rather ugly, but at least the authorities have forbidden the construction of both seafront high-rise hotels and any structures that don't blend in with the overall architecture of the area.

Tourism has greatly altered Hurghadah. When tourism in the Nile Valley was hit by fears of terrorism, many wily traders from Luxor moved

Map on page 84

Red Sea Attacks
Tourism along the Red Sea coast shows no signs of abating despite three large bombs being planted in tourist resorts in recent years. In 2004 a large bomb on the Sinai targetted Israeli tourists, 2005 saw another large explosion in Sharm al-Sheikh and in 2006 twenty people died when a bomb was planted in the popular resort of Dahab. You are still highly unlikely to come to harm but tourists should be aware of the dangers and keep their eyes open.

their operations here, an area which has hardly been affected by the problems. Hurghadah is all that many tourists see of Egypt; they often forget that they are in a Muslim country, and treat Hurghadah as if European mores prevail.

The present governor has plans to turn the whole Red Sea coast into one long beach and sports resort. However, there are ecological objections to such plans: many of the coral reefs have already been badly damaged by divers.

BEACH ACTIVITIES

The pleasures of Hurghadah itself are the ideal antidote to an overdose of monuments, of which it has none. The ★★**Red Sea Aquarium** (open daily 9am–10pm, closed Fri for prayers), on the Corniche in ad-Dahar district, contains examples of Red Sea fauna. Plaques provide detailed information.

For the divers and the fishermen, all-day or overnight diving and fishing trips to the islands can be arranged through the hotels. Squid, barracuda, exotic fish and coral can all be found near the surface. If you are not a diver, the *Sinbad* submarine submerges daily from 9am. Book at hotel reception desks (tel: 065-344 9601). The **Seascope** is a more modern glass-bottom boat that does two-hour trips (tel: 065-344 7974).

Though the beaches in Hurghadah are not exactly stunning, most of those owned by hotels

Translucent sea and coral

are well kept and offer plenty of watersports facilities. There is a public beach, though it is not recommended for unaccompanied women.

DIVING VILLAGES

Bur Safagah is half an hour's drive south of Hurghadah, and many divers consider it superior; the coral banks are more intact, and the small tourist resort and its hotels tend to attract tourists slightly more discerning than the masses in Hurghadah. With deepwater facilities, Bur Safagah is the nearest port to Qena, 177km (110 miles) to the west.

About 85km (53 miles) south of Bur Safagah is **Al-Qusayr**, an important harbour in ancient times as well as under Arab rule. Though this sleepy village now has several resort hotels, it offers a quieter alternative for divers.

Marsa Alam, 132km (82 miles) south of Al-Qusayr, is the latest fishing village to be developed for tourism. The diving and snorkelling is magnificent, and as yet unspoiled.

MOUNTAIN EXCURSION

★★**Mons Porphyritis**, the 'porphyry mountain', was the most important quarry in Roman times (30BC–AD395). Travel 18km (11 miles) north from Bur Safagah along the coast road onto a track which is easy to miss. It leads off towards the mountains, and 80km (50 miles) further is the old Roman quarry and town. This trip through rugged mountain scenery can be undertaken only with a four-wheel drive vehicle and is a real experience.

Mons Claudianus was another granite quarry valued by Roman emperors. Travel from Hurghadah towards Bur Safagah (31km/19 miles), and along the well-surfaced desert road towards Qena in the Nile Valley. Mons Claudianus is down a turn-off to the right. The round trip to Mons Claudianus from Hurghadah covers 200km (124 miles). Local tour operators also do one- and two-day trips by plane to the ★★**Monastery of St Catherine** (*see page 96*) in the Sinai.

Star Attractions
● **Red Sea Aquarium**
● **Mons Porphyritis**

The Red Sea is a diver's paradise

Dates growing at Siwah Oasis

10: Sun, Sea and Desert

Alexandria – Al-Alamayn – Marsa Matruh – Siwah Oasis

Whole worlds seem to separate Alexandria and the Siwah Oasis, although they're actually 604km (375 miles) apart. Alexandria *(see page 45)* is the cosmopolitan harbour city; the oasis of Siwah, in the middle of the Libyan Desert, has always been isolated (although a road currently under construction between Al-Baharivvah and Siwah is set to incorporate it into the desert circuit). Its inhabitants – of Berber descent – have developed their own independent culture which they are careful to protect today. On the right-hand side of the road from Alexandria to the Siwah Oasis are palm-lined beaches, beautiful bays and now also many unfinished resorts and holiday villages favoured by Egyptians. Across the road is the desert fringe.

EGYPTIAN RIVIERA

This route is best done by car; the bus tends to be rather time consuming and exhausting. Leave Alexandria on the desert road in the direction of Cairo, and turn off after 15km (9 miles) towards

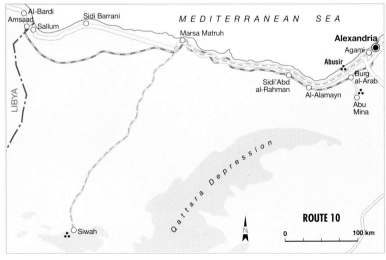

ROUTE 10

0   100 km

Agami. The well-paved road passes through an industrial area, then hugs the coast. At 106km (66 miles) into the trip, Al-Alamayn *(see page 50)* comes into view. The ★ **Egyptian Riviera** begins 46km (28 miles) east of Al-Alamayn, from **Sidi Abd al-Rahman** (150km/93 miles) onwards.

Star Attraction
● **Siwah Oasis**

THE ORACLE AND THE OASIS

Cleopatra built a palace near **Marsa Matruh** for herself and Mark Antony. Today the resort is popular with the Egyptian middle classes. A rock cave 3.5km (2 miles) out of town, where Cleopatra used to swim, is all that survives of her private beach.

Marsa Matruh is the gateway to the ★★ **Siwah Oasis**, famous in antiquity for its oracle of the Temple of Amun. Many powerful people were attracted to Aghurmi, its former main town. Alexander the Great heard that he would become lord of the world and a God here. Pilgrims from Greece travelled by boat and across the desert to hear the oracle.

Allow a good three hours for the 300km (186 mile) trip to the oasis (pop. 30,000), which lies 20m (66ft) below sea level and contains groves of palms, olives, oranges and dates, as well as vineyards and cornfields. It measures roughly 30km (18 miles) from north to south and 82km (51 miles) from east to west. Here, married women wear veils outside the home where they spend most of their time; in contrast, young, unmarried girls wear colourful dresses and their hair in plaits. Siwi is a separate, Berber language and the **Siwah Museum** (open 9am–noon, closed Fri) explores their culture.

Conquerors over the centuries have shown interest in subjugating Siwah but with little success. Cambyses the Persian arrived in the 6th century to burn the oracle's temple. His 50,000-strong army perished on its way across the desert, leaving no trace – not even a single skeleton.

Aghurmi was washed away by heavy rain in the 1920s. The ruins resemble haunted castles. The later capital of ★ **Shali** was founded in 1203. There are more than 200 springs in the Siwah Oasis, some of which you can bathe in. Nearby is the Great Sand Sea, with magnificent sand dunes and lakes.

> **Oracle's tricks**
> In 1994 the German Archaeological Institute in Cairo tried to prove the oracle was just a clever trick of the priests of the Temple of Amun: the building's acoustics were cleverly structured to produce echo effects – when a priest spoke in a hiding place, the walls amplified his voice.

The old town, Siwah

Map
below

11: Desert Oases

Cairo – Al-Bahariyyah – Al-Farafrah – Al-Dakhlah – Al-Khargah

It certainly takes far less time to reach Upper Egypt from Cairo on the main road than it does via this route, but the road that travels in a broad arc through the Libyan Desert is very impressive indeed. The prerequisite for this five-to-seven-day trip of around 1,000 km (621 miles) is a four-wheel drive vehicle, and it's best to travel with company. The tour can also be done by bus. *Before embarking on the journey, read the warning about safety on page 53.*

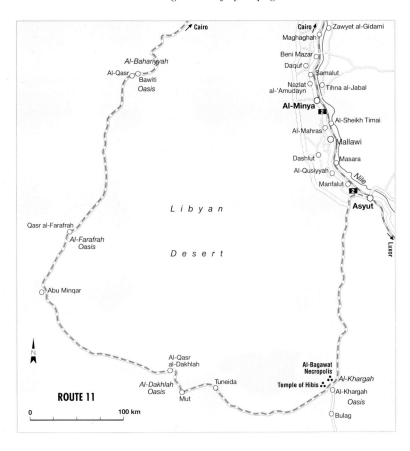

Cairo
Zawyet al-Gidami
Maghaghah
Beni Mazar
Daquf
Samalut
Nazlat al-'Amudayn
Tihna al-Jabal
Al-Bahariyyah
Al-Qasr
Bawiti Oasis
Al-Minya
Al-Sheikh Timai
Al-Mahras
Mallawi
Dashlut
Masara
Al-Qusiyyah
Nile
Manfalut
Asyut
L i b y a n
Qasr al-Farafrah
Al-Farafrah Oasis
D e s e r t
Luxor
Abu Minqar
Al-Qasr al-Dakhlah
Al-Bagawat Necropolis
Temple of Hibis
Al-Khargah
Al-Dakhlah Oasis
Tuneida
Al-Khargah Oasis
ROUTE 11
Mut
Bulag
N
0   100 km

The ancient Egyptians called the desert the 'Ocean of Fire', and even today it is regarded in popular superstition as the home of witches and evil spirits. Deep valleys, high sand dunes, rocky massifs and mountains lie along the route, which leads through the Qantara Valley. When Herodotus saw the Oasis of Al-Khargah in the 5th century BC, he called it 'the island of the blessed'.

AL-BAHARIYYAH OASIS

Leave Cairo at the Pyramids and travel the 360km (224 miles) to the ★★**Al-Bahariyyah Oasis** (162km/101 miles long, 42km/26 miles wide). This is the first oasis on the trip, with the main town of ★**Bawiti** surrounded by palm groves. Ancient traditions are all-important here, and far more powerful than any laws imposed from Cairo. Despite this, the oasis has seen an increasing number of tourists since the discovery in the 1990s of a cache of more than 100 painted mummies. The mummies are a reminder that Al-Bahariyyah thrived during the Greco-Roman period, famous for its wheat and wine. Two of the 'golden mummies' are on show at the antiquities inspectorate in Bawiti. A small mound in town known as **Qarat al-Firaji**, has several underground galleries for mummified sacred birds. There are also natural springs in and around town, though swimming, particularly for women, is not recommended. The best spot for bathing is about 15km (9 miles) north of Bawiti, at **Bir al-Ghaba**.

To the west of Bawiti is the **Temple of Alexander the Great**, but the images of Alexander have mostly worn away. The 26th-Dynasty **Temple of Ain al-Muftella** to the south of Bawiti has been extensively restored in recent years.

LAND OF THE COW

It's another 128km (79 miles) southwest to **Al-Farafrah Oasis**. During antiquity it was known as *Taihw*, or 'land of the cow', and was dedicated to the goddess Hathor. The oasis is 125km

Star Attraction
● Al-Bahariyyah Oasis

The White Desert
Just beyond Bawiti lies the Black Desert, so-called because it is covered in black stones, but the greatest attraction in the area is no doubt the White Desert, just before arriving at the oasis of Al-Farafrah. The White Desert has some amazing chalk rocks eroded by the strong wind into dramatic abstract sculptures. These change colour with the sun and turn from milk white into yellow golden and deep purple at sunset.

Setting off from Al-Bahariyyah Oasis

Map
on page
92

Below: Al-Dakhlah mosque
Bottom: high dunes in
the desert

(78 miles) long and 56km (35 miles) wide. The town of ★ **Qasr Al-Farafrah** is dominated by a fortress which, though inhabited, is crumbling through water erosion. A local artist, Badr, has a museum in a mudbrick house he built himself.

MUDBRICK VILLAGE

The desert road runs 313km (194 miles) between Al-Farafrah and the **Al-Dakhlah Oasis** (250sq km/96sq miles), which may have been inhabited for the past 10,000 years. Buffalo, elephants, rhinoceri and zebras used to live on the shore of a huge lake here. Today the oasis lives off its agricultural produce. The population is made up of Berbers and Bedouins, some of Libyan origin. A direct caravan route from Asyut had its terminus in the village of ★ **Balat**, where a hive of mudbrick dwellings testifies to medieval prosperity. Using only mud and straw, builders attained a sophistication that combines utility, beauty and harmony with the natural surroundings.

In the town of **Mut**, don't miss the small but excellent **Ethnological Museum** (the tourist office will open it for you). The oasis town of **Al-Qasr** has hot springs and is very picturesque.

AL-KHARGAH OASIS

About 200km (124 miles) further on is the ★★ **Al-Khargah Oasis**, 30km (19 miles) wide, 185km (115 miles) long and surrounded by hills. The town of Al-Khargah has several attractive old streets, and is the capital of the New Valley Governorate consisting of Al-Khargah, Al-Dakhlah and Al-Farafrah. Since 1983 attempts have been made to irrigate and industrialise the region. Just northeast of the town a cluster of monuments includes the **Temple of Hibis**, important as one of the few remnants of Persian rule, and the **Al-Bagawat** Coptic necropolis.

The well-surfaced road now leads 227km (141 miles) back into the Nile Valley to Asyut, and connects with the road to Luxor *(see page 54)* and the classic Nile Valley sightseeing route.

12: The Sinai Peninsula

Suez – Monastery of St Catherine – Nuwayba – Sharm al-Shaykh – Suez

The Sinai Peninsula is one of the most fascinating landscapes in Egypt. Created by continental drift, half the landscape is made up of granite mountains and is a sight to behold, with blue, green and red rock. The sea is also a more intense turquoise than in many other parts of the world. The Sinai is steeped in history: Christians believe God spoke to Moses here, and Christians and Jews alike used it as a place of refuge. Ancient trading routes also passed through the Sinai.

WESTERN SINAI

This route leads from the Gulf of Suez along a stretch of road full of bends and ravines, across the Sinai mountains to the Gulf of Aqaba. It requires at least three days and can be completed equally well by car, taxi or bus.

The starting-point is Suez *(see page 84)*. Then 32km (20 miles) south of the Ahmed Hamdi Tunnel is **'Uyun Musa**. The name means 'spring of Moses' and, according to the Bible, it was here during the flight from Egypt that Moses threw a tree into the brackish water of this spring and thus transformed it into drinking water.

Map on page 97

Star Attraction
● Al-Khargah Oasis

Nature parks
With the rapid development of tourism along the Sinai coast, it was decided in the 1990s to protect Egypt's precious natural areas. Ras Muhammad was the country's first National Park, with over 1000 different types of fish and 150 types of coral. The Tiran archipelago and the mangroves of Nabq near Dahab are now a nature reserve, while the St Catherine Protectorate protects both the natural assets of the area and the livelihood of the Bedouins. *(See page 116.)*

The rocky Sinai Mountains

The Library

The Library at the monastery of St Catherine has the most important collection of religious manuscripts after the Vatican. There are more than 5,000 rare books and 3,000 manuscripts, and the special permission needed to see them is hard to obtain. The monks are rightly suspicious. In the 19th century a German scholar stole one of their rarest manuscripts, Codex Sinaiticus. It came into the hands of the Czar of Russia, and the Communist regime later sold it to the British Museum where it remains to this day.

St Catherine's Monastery

After a further 143km (89 miles), turn left at Abu Rudis (175km/109 miles). It is generally believed that the ancient Israelites reached Mount Sinai via exactly this route. After 45km (28 miles), palm trees announce the oasis of Wadi Firan, which early Christians identified with exodus and Moses. They appointed a bishop and built a convent that was ruined in the 7th century. Archaeologists are excavating the old settlement and the ruins, but a new convent was built that depends on the monastery of St Catherine. The mountains around here are dotted with caves of hermits.

MONASTERY OF ST CATHERINE

The road continues through wide wadis for about 45km (28 miles) before reaching the Greek-Orthodox ★★★**Monastery of St Catherine**. (open Mon–Thur and Sat 9.30am–noon, closed Fri, Sun and Greek Orthodox religious holidays).

St Catherine was born in AD294 in Alexandria. She came from a wealthy family, was versed in philosophy, good at mathematics and spoke several languages. She was also a Christian, and her attempts to convert the pagan Roman Emperor Maxentius led to her death sentence.

She was executed on a spiked wheel, hence the Catherine wheel. This broke when she touched it, and when the emperor had her beheaded her body was taken by angels to Sinai. Tradition has it that priests found the remains of her body on Jabal Katerina, the highest peak in Egypt at 2,642m (8,668ft).

THE BURNING BUSH

The first chapel was built in AD337 for the Byzantine Empress Helena, not for St Catherine, on the site of the Burning Bush that spoke to Moses, which had become a centre for pilgrims. After repeated attacks by nomadic tribes, the Emperor Justinian ordered for a fortified basilica and monastery to be built in AD537, which was to be protected by two hundred guards.

The building is situated 1,528m (5,013ft) above sea level in a mountain valley. The monks were driven out of the monastery several times from the 7th to 18th centuries. The Prophet Muhammad guaranteed their protection, but there were very few monks until St Catherine's remains were found, and then the monastery was dedicated to her. To prevent the monastery's destruction after the Islamisation of Egypt in the 10th century, a mosque was built next to it. Now there are just over 20 monks, most from Mt Athos in Greece.

Star Attractions
● **Monastery of St Catherine**
● **basilica**

BASILICA FRESCO

The highlight of the labyrinthine monastery area is the magnificent three-aisled ★★**basilica**: note the

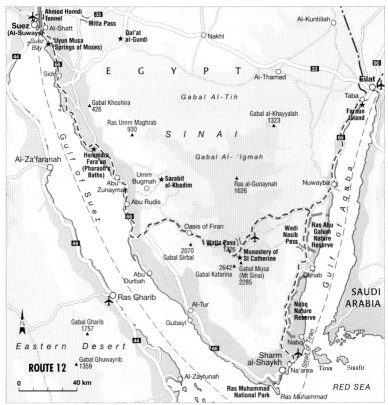

Map
on page
97

Below: monastery bell tower
Bottom: an acacia tree in the
Sinai Desert

superb fresco above the main altar in the dome showing the transfiguration of Christ. The prophet Elijah (left) and Moses (right) can be seen on either side of Jesus; beneath him, still sleepy, is Peter (with John and Jacob directly above him). The whole scene is framed by medallions. The two golden caskets next to the marble shrine of St Catherine contain the hand and head of the saint. Beyond the choir is the ★ **Chapel of the Burning Bush**, built on the site where God is said to have appeared to Moses. It measures only 3m (10ft) by 5m (16ft); the altar is supported by four slender marble columns.

MOUNT MOSES

Another popular pilgrimage destination nearby is to climb ★★ **Jabal Musa** (Mount Moses/Mount Sinai) at dawn or sunset. This is where Moses is supposed to have received the tablets bearing the Ten Commandments. There are 3,400 granite steps leading to the top of the 2,285m (7,497ft) mountain. There is also a camel path and two-thirds of the trip up can be done on a camel. Although the climb has become increasingly popular, often with crowds on the top, the view of the sun setting or coming up over these glorious bare mountains is still a solemn moment, particularly when Muslims, Christians and Jews pray together.

NORTHERN ROUTE

The road along the Gulf of Aqaba comes into view 75km (47 miles) further on. There are now two alternative routes: north or south.

The northern option leads 37km (23 miles) along the coast to **Nuwayba**. This town used to be popular with backpackers. Today mass tourism has arrived and this little town, with its palm-lined beaches and coral reefs, has several hotels and clubs. Along the coast road are villages of straw-thatched huts where freshly caught fish can be eaten and seaside accommodation is cheap. Another 107km (66 miles) further on is the border town of **Taba**, next to Israel's Eilat. It consists of little more than the Taba Hilton and several other luxury developments. Lying 200m (656ft) offshore is **Faraun Island** with a ruined fortress, built by Saladin in the 12th century.

SOUTHERN ROUTE

The coast road leads from the Monastery of St Catherine to **Dahab**, 37km (23 miles) away. Like Nuwayba, the former Bedouin village of Dahab used to be a popular backpackers' destination. It is still the most laid-back of the Sinai resorts.

Continue for 137km (85 miles) along the coast to reach Egypt's famous tourist resort of ★ **Sharm al-Shaykh**. Luxury hotels and expensive clubs here cater for the European divers and sun-worshippers, mainly Italians. The prices are high, and it can feel like a resort anywhere in the world. The main hotel area is on Na'ama Bay, beside some of the best diving in the region (*see page 115*).

Mass tourism has brought a host of problems. Coral banks have been destroyed, either by souvenir-hungry divers or damage by ships' anchors, and the nearby **Ras Muhammad National Park**, now Egypt's first natural park, has had ecological problems. Several hotels get their drinking water delivered in tankers three times a day from sea-water desalination plants, and sewage is pumped straight into the sea. Tourism is growing faster than the infrastructure to deal with it.

Star Attraction
● **Gebel Musa**
(Mount Moses/
Mount Sinai)

Coral reefs
The coral reefs of Southern Sinai are truly amazing. Often, and particularly in Sharm al-Shaykh, you can just snorkel off the beach and see an amazing variety of fishes and corals. However, there are even greater thrills to be had for those who go diving further off shore. Common sights are yellow anemone fish, parrot fish, damsel fish, scorpion fish, stingrays, dolphins, Napoleon fish, barracuda and shark.

Ras Muhammad National Park

Ancient Egypt and the Arts

RELIGION IN ANCIENT EGYPT

The ancient Egyptians believed that life continued after death. Even though the body died, the soul lived on in the afterworld, which was a mirror-image of this world and in which the *ka*, or life force, returned to the body.

It was the duty of the relatives to secure a decent life in the hereafter for their loved one by filling the tomb with burial gifts, otherwise there was a danger that the person would 'return with the wind' and take revenge on them. The tomb was the home of the deceased, and was not complete without the *Book of the Dead*, which contained magic formulae to ward off danger. The ancient Egyptians also believed that one's rank in life remained the same after death; thus a pharaoh could not become an official, or vice versa.

Unlike men, however, the gods could change their form at will. Many were represented as animals, such as cats, cows or bulls. The god Sobek had the head of a crocodile, and the goddess Hathor the head of a cow.

Religious beliefs were accompanied by a number of opposed dualities. Chaos, the watery waste preceding the creation of the world, was followed by the orderly cosmos. The same deities often embodied apparent contradictions: Osiris, for instance, was the god of the dead and also the god of fertility. Death and life followed each other in the same way as the sun rose and set.

This life and the hereafter were in opposing directions, with the living in the east and the 'beautiful dead' in the west. Thus Luxor, on the Nile's eastern bank, was the world of life and god-worship, while the pharaohs set off on their journey into the afterworld from Thebes on the west bank.

MUMMIFICATION

From 3400BC, the elaborate art of mummification served to prepare the body for its journey into the afterworld and to preserve it for all

Ancient deities

Amun: god of Thebes and of the sun, shown as a man with two plumes, crook and flail.

Anubis: a god of the dead, shown as a jackal, or as a man with a jackal's head.

Apis: god of fertility and death, shown as a bull with sun disk; Ptah's sacred animal.

Aten: god of the sun, shown as a rayed disk, the rays terminating in hands.

Bastet: goddess of love and joy, depicted as a cat.

Bes: domestic god, protector of women in childbirth, shown as a dwarf.

Khnum: creator god, represented as a man with a ram's head.

Hathor: goddess of love and dancing, shown as a cow-headed woman with a horned headdress.

Horus: god of the sky and of light, shown as a falcon.

Imhotep: deified chief of works of King Zoser of the 3rd Dynasty, shown as a seated man holding papyrus.

Isis: mother goddess and protector of the dead, shown as a woman with a throne upon her head.

Osiris: god of the afterworld, vegetation and fertility, shown as a human mummy with feathered crown and beard.

Ptah: creator god of Memphis, represented as a mummified man.

Re: sun god of Heliopolis, shown as a man with a falcon's or ram's head.

Thoth: moon god of Hermopolis, and scribe and vizier of the gods, shown with the head of an ibis or sometimes a baboon.

Opposite: the Sphinx

Osiris the judge

Scenes in ancient Egyptian tombs often show the deceased's heart being weighed against the goddess Maat's Feather of Truth, for the Judgement of Osiris. The god Anubis is in charge of the scales, while Thoth records the verdict. The guilty were devoured by the crocodile-headed Ammut, while the righteous were led by Osiris to their resurrection. The Underworld consisted of 12 gates, like the 12 hours that the Sun disappeared in the underworld between sunset and dawn.

Hieroglyphs in Luxor Museum

eternity. The amount of care taken in the procedure depended on the rank and wealth of the deceased. Mummification of the highest ranking, for example, took a full 70 days. The mummies of pharaohs thus remained preserved for centuries, and the greatest danger to them wasn't so much the passage of time as visits by tomb-robbers – and by archaeologists such as Howard Carter. The mummy of Tutankhamun broke into pieces when archaeologists and doctors tried to examine it.

Embalmers first drained and disembowelled the corpse and pulled out the brain through the nose, with the aid of a hook. They then cut open the lower part of the body at the side to drain it. Internal organs were then extracted to prevent putrefaction, and the intestines were cleaned, wrapped in bandages and placed in canopic jars next to the tomb; the only organ left inside the body was the heart. Blocks of natron placed around the body absorbed fat and water. Cheaper methods involved the introduction of acidic soda solutions into the bowels, which was sluiced out again once the intestines had dissolved.

The treatment with natron disfigured the body: cheeks became sunken, and muscles vanished. Retaining the body's original appearance became a fine art. Experiments were also carried out with sawdust and various fats that might pad out shrunken tissue. Over the centuries this gradually expanded and eventually split the skin open.

The last phase of mummification involved wrapping the entire body with strips of perfumed linen. These were soaked in oils and resins which later dyed the mummies a dark brown. Amulets and inscriptions such as 'May death strike all who disturb the peace of the Pharaoh' were wrapped inside the bandages to protect the deceased.

During the Middle Ages it was widely believed that Egyptian mummies were prepared with bitumen, which was supposed to have a medicinal value. 'Mummy' potion was made by pounding mummified bodies and was a standard product of apothecary shops. The traffic in mummies continued in Europe until the 18th century.

Research on mummies is only just beginning but recent CT scans and DNA analyses have rendered some insights. The genetic information reveals that hashish and other drugs, bilharzia and malnutrition disorders (resulting from the frequent famines) were common in ancient Egypt.

ANCIENT EGYPTIAN ART

The primary purpose of art in pharaonic times was to serve the gods. Pyramids, temples, graves, wall paintings, statues and reliefs were all dedicated to the pharaoh, who represented the connection between gods and men.

Egyptian painting, with its lack of perspective, strove to remain true to reality by concentrating on essentials. The wall paintings reveal much about life in ancient Egypt. Some paintings are delightful, such as the graceful images of flute, harp and lute players in the tomb of Nakht, priest of Amun.

Imhotep (c2665BC), King Zoser's chief of works, who built the Step Pyramid at Saqqarah, is considered the father of stone architecture. At that time temples were still an integral part of pyramid burial sites. Later on, pyramids gave way to tombs cut into the rock to conceal them from robbers, and even though these temples lay at some distance from the tombs themselves, they increased in importance. These sacred structures

Below: a wall painting of Anubis from the Valley of the Kings
Bottom: the Hypostyle Hall in the Temple of Karnak

were made of stone, while profane buildings, whether huts or palaces, were built merely of clay.

COPTIC ART

The new religion of Christianity evoked popular art forms strongly influenced by the heritage of pharaonic and Graeco-Roman art. Further inspiration was provided by Byzantium. After the 4th century, themes from Greek and Roman mythology were invariably replaced by Christian motifs. It is, however, striking how the pictures of Coptic art often possess very clear ancient Egyptian characteristics. The holy cross of Christianity, for example, was on a par with the pharaonic *ankh* hieroglyph, meaning life, which was chosen as the symbol of Christ by the early Copts. Both crosses are often flanked by the alpha and omega, symbolising the beginning and end of all things. In frescoes and icons, biblical scenes were adapted to the ancient Egyptian heritage. Isis with Horus as a boy became Mary and child, and the Holy Spirit is represented by a bird with broad wings that embodied the soul of the deceased in the pharaonic death cult. The pillared arcades in the ancient Egyptian temples provided the inspiration for the earliest basilicas. The bright colours that survive are very cheerful, such as those in the Church of St Macarius in the Wadi Natrun monastery. The artists' love of detail and ornament formed a transition to Islamic art.

Many examples of Coptic art have been lost over the years – not least because of archaeologists. With their minds firmly fixed on ancient Egypt, they had several pharaonic reliefs featuring Coptic motifs removed without copying or photographing them for posterity. Champollion, who deciphered the Rosetta Stone, discovered a superbly preserved 5th-century church in Thebes, but his official report makes no mention of it.

ISLAMIC ART

Islamic art is religious art and can only be properly understood by the Christian beholder if he or

---

The Star of the Orient
The Egyptian singer Umm Kalthoum (1898–1975) occupies a very special place in the hearts of most Arabs. Her voice was extraordinary but with her songs she touched people in many ways. The ambiguous lyrics, where she often talked about subliminal love for God, expressed exactly what ordinary Egyptians felt for each other but were not necessarily allowed to say. On the first Thursday of every month she gave concerts that were attended by many and watched by millions on television. Her museum in Cairo *(see page 37)* is a place of pilgrimage.

The legendary Umm Kalthoum

she puts aside preconceived ideas about religious art. The most important principle governing art in the Islamic world is *aniconism*, that is the religious prohibition of the figurisation and representation of living creatures. This applies to the Prophet Muhammad and all other protagonists of the faith (saints in the Christian sense are unknown in Islam).

A magnificent and masterful art of ornamental decoration thus developed. During the 10th century the Fatimids made use of many gifted Coptic artists to give artistic expression to the Islamic religion. Calligraphy was considered the highest form of art, and still is today. Travellers to Egypt will frequently see the single word *Allah* written in gold letters and framed. In decorative art, colours, arabesques and plant motifs have replaced the human figure.

This is most evident in mosques, which are places not only of congregation for religious services but also quiet spaces of meditation for believers and – like Al-Azhar Mosque – centres of learning for students of the Koran. The most distinctive feature of mosques is their sheer size; their dimensions are massive. The ground-plan has remained unchanged for 1,300 years: arcades (*livan*) surround a large inner courtyard (*san*) with a fountain (*hanafija*). Handmade carpets hang from the walls. The architecture integrates

Below: the Bab Zuweila in Cairo
Bottom: the interior of the Alabaster Mosque

Alexandria's new library

functionality with religious proscriptions. From the tall and narrow minaret, the *muezzin* calls the faithful to prayer. A semicircular niche *(mihrab)* is reserved for the prayer leader *(imam)*, and points in the direction of Mecca *(kibla)*. The preacher *(khatib)* delivers sermons from his pulpit *(minbar)*, a seat at the top of steps near the *mihrab*.

MODERN ART

The ancient Egyptian, Coptic and Islamic heritage weighs heavily on present-day art. Over the past 200 years, art in Egypt has constantly striven to create some identity of its own: should it ignore its pharaonic heritage, develop it further or vary it? This confusion still exists today.

The sculptor Mahmud Mukhtar (1883–1934) saw art as an expression of national sentiment, and from 1921 the nationalists embraced his theories. He introduced the concept of neo-pharaonic art, which drew inspiration from various styles. After 17 centuries, Mukhtar was the first Egyptian sculptor to enjoy any success. He used the pink granite so valued by the pharaohs for his famous *Egypt Awakes* statue that stands outside the University of Cairo.

Other Modernist artists included Muhammad Nagui and the now widely recognised Mahmoud Said. Contemporary artists, such as Adel el-Siwi and the Armenian Chant Avedissian, continue to be inspired by traditional Egyptian themes, both folkloric and pharaonic, but are reaching much wider audiences.

Egyptian modern architecture seems to be the least concerned with the country's heritage: in the big cities, skyscrapers with mirror-glass facades stand beside buildings in British colonial or ornamental Arab style. Some 4,500 years of history have produced a complex mixture of domestic and foreign styles. Preserving what already exists is currently causing problems. 'Ruinist' was one critic's term for the prevailing architectural style of many of Egypt's modern buildings.

One exception to this was the Egyptian architect Hassan Fathy (1900–89), who was horrified by the development of concrete and red-brick villages, and strived for re-introducing mud-brick houses, which are much better adapted to the climate and more pleasing to the eye. At the time his ideas seemed perhaps too avant-garde, but some of his pupils including Olivier Sednaoui are continuing his good work.

Festivals

There are many Islamic festivals, and the Egyptians love celebrations. The official public holidays *(see page 121)* are also fascinating for tourists.

Egypt's three calendars (Gregorian, Islamic and Coptic) mean the year is filled with holidays. And when Egyptians celebrate, they make as much noise as they can. Births, weddings, send-offs for pilgrimages to Mecca and even funerals are very raucous affairs.

The festival of *Sham en-Nessim* ('smelling the west wind') celebrates the beginning of spring, and has its roots in the pharaonic Opet festival. It falls on Coptic Easter Monday.

Another famous Cairo festival has nothing to do with religion: the International Film Festival. American and other international stars open the

Below: the writer Ahdaf Soueif
Bottom: men at Daraw Camel Market

festival in December. Many of the 200 or so films from around 50 countries (especially Arab countries and Asia) have English or French subtitles.

Below: Friday prayers at Cairo's Al-Husayn Mosque
Bottom: selling vegetables on the street in Cairo

RAMADAN – FASTING AND FEASTING

The fast during the month of Ramadan is one of the Five Pillars of Islam. Every believer (with the exception of the sick, the old, children and pregnant or menstruating women) should comply with it. From sunrise to sunset eating and drinking, smoking and all sensual and physical pleasures, including sex, are forbidden. Life in Ramadan may be sleepy during the day, but the moment the sun sets the whole country turns into one big folk festival. The moment the cannon shot sounds the end of the fast (the Cairo cannon, known familiarly as the *Haqa Fatma*, stands on the Citadel), feasting commences. In the city's squares, children play on swing boats and hand-operated roundabouts, and set off home-made firecrackers. The high point of the month of fasting is the 26th night known as *Lailet al-Qadr* – the night when Muhammad received his first revelation from the archangel Gabriel.

Like all Islamic festivals, Ramadan's 30 days are derived from the Muslim lunar calendar, which dates from 15 July AD622, the day that Muhammad began his flight from Mecca to Medina. Officially Ramadan begins with the sighting of the sickle moon; if conditions are cloudy it can be delayed, sometimes for up to three days.

Ramadan ends with the 3-day *Aid al-Fitr*, but the most important Islamic festival is the *Aid al-Aolha* (Holy Days of Sacrifice). This takes place at the end of the Islamic year and recalls Abraham's willingness to sacrifice his son Ishmael. Muslims slaughter a sheep in his memory.

MAWLIDS – BIRTHDAY CELEBRATIONS OF HOLY FIGURES

For centuries the lives of revered religious figures have been remembered with colourful, fair-like celebrations. Such occasions – there are around

80 in Cairo alone – are known in Arabic as *mawlid*. These celebrations are actually frowned upon by some Muslims, who consider them to be idolatrous.

The sheiks of Cairo's Al-Azhar Mosque hold this opinion, but outside the Al-Husayn Mosque, opposite Al-Azhar, devout Muslims, dancing Sufis and mystics all celebrate the birthday of the Prophet Muhammad, as well as commemorating the martyrdom of Husayn with a festival lasting six days.

In early October, there are particularly lavish celebrations held in honour of the mystic Sayed Ahmed al-Badawi in Tanta on the Nile delta, the town where he died in 1273. Many thousands of people celebrate the miracle worker with a week-long oriental fair, involving snake charmers, horse ballets and whirling dervishes. The *mawlid* held at the Abu al-Haggag mosque in Luxor dates back to a pharaonic procession.

The *mawlids* are Egypt's true carnivals, both spiritual and fun. Pushcarts hawking everything from plastic machine-guns to chick peas sprout overnight, vying for space with the tents and sleeping bodies of country pilgrims. On the big night, while sufis dance to the rhythms of the *dhikr* (chanting to the remembrance of God), local kids try out the swings, shooting galleries and assorted tests of strength.

> ### Egyptian time
> Many Egyptians have a very different attitude to time than Westerners. Often when you need something done, you will hear that you can come back *inshallah bukra*, which literally means 'if God wants it tomorrow', but in effect means some indeterminate time in the future. Whatever happens you will hear them say *maalesh* when you may be getting very upset; this means anything from 'no problem' to 'no worries' or 'never mind' – even if disaster has just struck.

A rural mawlid

FOOD AND DRINK

MAIN DISHES

The upper classes in ancient Egypt consumed vast quantities of poultry, fish, vegetables, fruit and bread, washing it down with beer, wine and water. Economic necessity has meant that a lot of today's Egyptians are almost vegetarians. A teacher's income, barely above the statistical average, rarely allows the purchase of meat. For many, breakfast, lunch and supper consist of pitta bread *(aysh balladi)*, broad beans *(fuul)* and vegetable fritters *(tamiyya)*, which are delicious and available on nearly every street corner. Another popular form of fast food is the skewered meat similar to doner kebab known as *shawarma*.

Small, inexpensive restaurants often have only one speciality, such as spicy noodles with onion and lentils *(kushari),* which are well worth trying. Many dishes are flavoured with sesame seeds: dried beef wrapped in aromatic herbs *(pasterma)*, aubergine purée with sesame paste and garlic *(babaghanoug)*, aubergines marinated in garlic *(betingan)*, a delicious hard cheese *(gibnah rumi)* and the oily sesame paste, *tehina*. Pitta bread can be dunked into all these dips.

Other dishes that really should be tasted include a spicy cheese and tomato salad *(gibnah bi tamatem)*, and the pickled vegetable dishes known as *turshi* or *makhalil*, which most commonly consist of onions, shallots, carrots or olives with lemon. Another tasty vegetable dish is ladies' fingers with tomato sauce *(bamia)*. Dishes containing offal are also popular (raw camel liver is a rare delicacy).

Opinions tend to differ about *molucheyyah*, a thick soup made of something resembling spinach served with chicken or rabbit, but lentil soup flavoured with lemon *(shurbet ads)* is universally popular. There's less variation in the main courses based on meat: beef or lamb is usually grilled in the form of meatballs *(kofta)* or skewered *(kebab)* – both introduced during the long Turkish occupation of Egypt. Quail and stuffed pigeon *(hamam mahshi)* are delicious.

PUDDINGS

The desserts tend to be very sugary: flaky pastry with almonds and syrup *(baklava)*, wheat shredded with nuts, honey and sugar *(konafa)* or pastries filled with cream cheese *(atayyef)*. Less sweet than these is the rice pudding with rose-water and pistachios known as *mahalabiyyah*. Special desserts are eaten to celebrate the end of Ramadan and during other major festivals. *Umm Ali* is a typical Egyptian dessert of crisp pitta bread soaked in hot milk, with coconut, cream, nuts, raisins and sugar. Chocolates from Alexandria are famous, as are the cakes from Dumyat, on the eastern side of the Nile delta.

DRINKS

Orange, lemon, mango, carrot and guava juice are usually served fresh when in season. Many restaurants and all major hotels serve alcoholic drinks. A tasty local beer is *Stella Local*; better and more expensive is *Sakkara*. Local wines are usually table wines; among the best are *Omar Khayyam* (red), *Cru des Ptolemées* and also *Rubis d'Egypte* (rosé), and the Obelisque wines made from imported grapes. In 2005, Egypt launched its first vintage wine, *Château des Rêves*. Those watching their weight should order medium-sweet coffee *(akwa masbut)*, lightly sugared tea *(shai sukkar khafief)* or even unsugared tea *(shai menrir sukkar)*.

The hookah *(shisha)* is also listed as a beverage in Arabic and is best smoked apple-flavoured *(tofaha)*.

One word of warning: when buying mineral water, make sure the cap is undamaged. Bottles ordered in restaurants should be opened only at the table by the waiter, otherwise there's a good chance they contain tap-water.

Trendy hubbly bubbly
Many trendy Lebanese or Egyptian restaurants now serve *shishas* (hookahs) with or after the food. The smoke is believed to work as a digestive, and is a relaxing way to round off a meal.

Restaurant selection

The following are some of the better eateries in Egypt's main cities and resorts. You should book ahead for most of them. €€€ = expensive, €€ = moderate and € = cheap.

Alexandria

Adoura, 33 Bayram at-Tonsi. Great fish restaurant in a side street with al fresco dining. Fish comes with *mezze*, but no alcohol available. €€
Cap d'Or, 4 Sh Adib, off Sh Saad Zaghlul, tel: (03) 483 5177. Charming Art Nouveau bar with cold beers and sizzling seafood *mezze*. €–€€
Les Ambassadeurs, Metropole Hotel, Sh Saad Zaghlul, tel: (03) 486 1465. The best restaurant in downtown Alexandria with superior French-European cuisine. €€€
Samakmak, 42 Kasr Ras al-Tin, Al-Bahry, tel: (03) 481 1560. Excellent fish and seafood. €€€
Seagull, Al-Maqs, tel: (03) 440 5575. Excellent fish and seafood in a mock castle setting. €€€
Trianon, Sh Saad Zaghlul, Ramleh Station, tel: (03) 486 0986. Old-style café/cake shop. €

Aswan

Aswan Moon, Corniche, tel: (097) 231 6108. A good place for traditional Egyptian food. €
Chef Khalil, Sharia al Suq, tel: (097) 231 0142. A lovely, popular restaurant that serves fresh fish from Lake Nasser and the Red Sea. All fish dishes come with good French Fries and salads. €€
Nubian House Restaurant, about 1km (½ mile) south of Nubian Museum, on the river bank, tel: (097) 232 6226. Excellent folkloric show. €€

Cairo

Abu el-Sid, off 26th-of-July Street, Zamalek, tel: (02) 2735 9640. Great Egyptian restaurant, where tasty national specialities and waterpipes are served in an eclectic décor. €€
After Eight, 6 Sharia Qasr al-Nil, tel: (02) 2574 0855. A renovated night haunt serving Mediterranean and Middle Eastern dishes. The real attraction is the live jazz on most nights. €€
Andrea's, 59–60 Marioutiya Canal near the Giza Pyramids, tel: (02) 3383 1133. Outdoor restaurant with *mezze*, chicken, kebabs and cold beer too. Perfect for lunch after the pyramids. €€
Americana Fish Market, Americana boat, 26 Sharia an-Nil, Giza, tel: (02) 3570 9694. Excellent fish restaurant on a moored boat on the Nile. Select your fish and get it served with home-made bread and Middle Eastern salads. €€
La Bodega Lounge, 157, 26th-of-July Street, Zamalek, tel: (02) 2735 6761. Beautifully restored from a 1920s Cairo apartment into a brasserie, a lounge and bar. The décor is Japanese-inspired and the cuisine is a fabulous fusion or Mediterranean brasserie food. €€€
Felfela, 15 Sh Hoda Sharawi, city-centre, tel: (02) 2392 2833. Popular Egyptian. €€
Fishawi Coffee-House, near Al-Husayn Mosque, Khan al-Khalili. Traditional teahouse, open 24 hours. €

Marriottt Garden, Cairo Marriott Hotel Sh Saraya al-Gezira, Zamalek, tel: (02) 2735 8888. The garden terrace offers perfect refuge from hectic Cairo, either for a drink or for a casual meal. €€

Moghul Room, tel: (02) 383 3222. Top quality Indian food with soothing live music served in a cosy but plush décor. €€€

Naguib Mahfouz Coffee Shop 5 Sikket al-Badestan, main alley in Khan al-Khalili, tel: (02) 2590 3788. A haven in the main souk area with fresh juices, Egyptian sweets and waterpipes, or good Egyptian food in the restaurant. €–€€

Seasons, Four Seasons Hotel, 35 Sh Giza, tel: (02) 3573 1212. A grand and elegant restaurant that serves Egyptian specialities with a twist, as well as superb international cuisine. €€€

Sabaya, Semiramis InterContinental, Corniche al-Nil, Garden City, tel: (02) 2795 7171. Delicious and elegant restaurant that serves a refined and very fresh Lebanese cuisine in contemporary Oriental decor. €€€

Hurghadah

Da Nanni, Resort strip, Sigala, tel: (065) 344 7018. The best pizza in town made by an Italian couple. €€

Felfella, Sharia Sheraton, tel: (065) 344 2410. Decent Egyptian food served at tables with views over the Red Sea. €–€€

Papa's Bar, Next door to Pizza Rossi, Sigala, tel: (010) 512 9051. A lively bar in the heart of Sigala, popular with local residents and dive instructors, who party here at weekends. €

Luxor

Al Moudira, Daba'iyya, 5km (3 miles) south of ticket office on the West Bank, tel: (012) 325 1307. Worth the excursion both for the architecture and atmosphere of the hotel, and for the delicious food served by the beautiful poolside or indoors. €€€

La Mamma, Sheraton Sharia Khaled ibn el-Walid, tel: (095) 237 4544. Good Italian dishes served in the pleasant garden. €€

Nur al-Gurna, opposite the ticket office, Al-Qurnah, tel: (095) 231 1430. Simple restaurant in a pleasant shady garden that serves local dishes such as stews, *meloukhiya*, roast duck and stuffed pigeon, but no alcohol. €–€€

Oasis Café, off the Corniche an-Nil, behind the Mercure Hotel, tel: (095) 237 2914. Set in an Italianate villa with high ceilings and Islamic furniture, this is the perfect place for a drink, lunch or casual dinner. 1940s jazz is in the air. €–€€

Sharm al-Shaykh

Abu el-Sid, Na'ama Bay, tel: (069) 360 3910. Atmospheric place in Oriental décor, above Hard Rock Café. Good local food in a/c interior or on outside terrace. €€

Felfela, Old Sharm Market. Great local Egyptian food. Try *shakshouka* for starters and *Om Ali* for dessert. €

La Rustichella, Behind Na'ama Bay, tel: (010) 116 0692. Very popular Italian restaurant with plenty of fish and seafood, as *la mamma* cooks it. €€

Tam Tam, Ghazala Hotel on the beachfront, tel: (069) 360 0150. Tasty Egyptian food and fresh juices. €€–€€€

Siwah

Dunes, Just off the central square, on the road to Gebel Dakrour, Siwah town, tel: (010) 653 0372. Great restaurant-bar with a large menu including all the Siwan and Egyptian specialities, as well as *shishas* and Siwan music. €

Kenooz, Sh Seboukha, Siwah town, tel: (046) 460 2399. Excellent Egyptian and Siwan food served on a pleasant terrace under the stars and the palm trees. $–$$

NIGHTLIFE

OPERA IN CAIRO

The Opera on Gezira, tel: (02) 2739 0114, www.cairoopera.org, is Egypt's only opera house. It has regular guests from abroad but also stages its own productions. The programme ranges from Mozart (in Arabic) and ballet to evenings of Arabic music. Phone bookings are not possible; tickets are on sale at the Opera House from 9am to 2pm.

BARS
Cairo

Bam-Bu Lounge Club, Casino al-Shagara, tel: (02) 2579 6511, Corniche an-Nil, Bulaq opposite the World Trade Centre. Next door to Sangria, very lively on Thursday and Saturday nights. €€
Morocco Nile City boat, Corniche Al-Nil, Zamalek, tel: (02) 2735 3314. Moroccan restaurant and bar-disco overlooking the Nile; now one of Cairo's hottest nightspots. €€€
Le Tabasco, Maydan Amman, Dokki, tel: (02) 3336 5583. €€
Windsor Bar, 19 Sharia Alfy, Downtown, tel: (02) 2591 5277. Colonial-style old bar with ancient waiters and dusty peanuts, but good cold beers. €–€€
White, 19 Sharia Hassan Asem, Zamalek, tel: (012) 230 4404. Trendy very white bar in a basement, with some of the latest music in town and very good-looking waiters. €€

> **Door policy**
> More upmarket discos or lounges may refuse entry if you are dressed too casually or in jeans. Egyptians are never knowingly underdressed, particularly the women. Some places also have a couples-only policy to avoid trouble, although single foreign women will usually be let in.

DISCOTHEQUES

All the major hotels in the main tourist centres have their own discos. The big nights out are Thursday and Friday.

Cairo

Exit, Atlas Hotel, Sharia Mohammed Rushdy, Downtown. €–€€
Latex, Nile Hilton Hotel, Corniche al-Nil, Downtown, tel: (02) 2578 0666. The place to be seen in town. €€€
Rithmo, Semiramis InterContinental, Corniche an-Nil, Garden City, tel: (02) 2795 7171. €€€

Hurghadah

Dome, InterContinental Hotel, tel: (065) 344 6911. A favourite.
Ministry of Sound, Papas Beach Club, Sigala, tel: (012) 329 7530, www.ministryofsoundegypt.com. Theme parties every night.

Luxor

El-Sarab Bar, Hotel Mercure Sharia al-Karnak, tel: (095) 237 4944. Belly dance show and disco. €€
Tutotel, Sharia Salah ad-Din, near the Novotel, tel: (095) 237 7990. Most popular disco in town. €€

NIGHTCLUBS
Cairo

Places *not* recommended to go are the establishments along the Sh al-Haram (Pyramids Road) in Giza. These clubs charge tourists extortionate prices.

The following nightclubs are recommended, though they're not cheap: **Empress**, Marriott Hotel, Corniche al-Nil, Zamalek, tel: (02) 2735 8888 (€€€); **Alhambra,** Cairo Sheraton, tel: (02) 2336 9700 (€€€); **Abu Nanas**, Mene House Hotel, tel: (02) 3383 3222 (€€). For belly dancing try the seedier **Palmyra** in an alley off 26th-of-July Street downtown (€).

ACTIVE HOLIDAYS

DIVING AND SNORKELLING

The Red Sea resort towns of Hurghadah, Al-Qusayr and Bur Safagah, and Sharm al-Shaykh on the southern tip of Sinai are all ideal for water sports such as surfing, diving, snorkelling, water-skiing and jet-skiing. The most exciting areas for divers are between Sharm al-Shaykh (Na'ama Bay) and Dahab: the famous Jackson Reef with its steep walls and black coral, the Blue Hole, and – only for real experts – the Canyon and the Tower, with overhangs and steep drops of 80m (262ft) or more. Divers' knives are forbidden in the Sinai, with good reason: far too much coral has been damaged. Bringing coral back to land is strictly forbidden. Captains of vessels who take coral-collectors out to sea lose their licence if caught.

Diving and snorkelling courses can be booked via hotels or clubs. In Sharm al-Shaykh contact Shark's Bay Diving, tel: (069) 360 0942; www.sharksbay.com or the Red Sea Diving College (instruction only, with student accommodation), tel: (069) 360 0145; www.redseacollege.com. For diving in the eastern harbour in Alexandria contact Alexandra Dive, tel: (03) 483 2045; www.alexandra-dive.com.

SURFING

The best place for surfers is Hurghadah, where a good breeze blows nearly every day. Two of the best areas are Magawish and Hurghadah Beach. Surfboards can be hired from several surf centres for around £100 a week.

FISHING

Fishing is allowed everywhere – from the Corniche in Alexandria or on fishing boats. The latter can be rented at the harbour near Alexandria's Fort Qaytbay. Organised fishing trips are available in the Red Sea, and boats can also be hired for private trips. Fishing safaris on Lake Nasser are increasingly popular. Contact **African Angler**, tel: (097) 230 9748; www.africanangler.co.uk or **Wild Nuba**, fax: (097) 232 3636; www.lakenasseradventure.com for safaris in search of the giant Nile Perch which weigh up to 100kg (220lb).

GOLF

Dreamland Golf resort, Wahat Road, Dreamland City, Cairo, tel: (02) 3855

A dervish show in Cairo

3164; www.dreamlandgolf.com. 18-hole course with views over the Pyramids. **El Gouna Golf**, tel: (065) 258 0009; www.elgouna.com. USPGA-sized 18-hole championship course.

RIDING

It is best to hire horses only from one of the renowned stables. In the village near the Sphinx, Nazlet al-Semaan, the best stables are **AA**, tel: (02) 3385 0531, and **MG**, tel: (02) 3385 1241. According to local riders, the best stable of all is the **International Equestrian Club**, on Saqqara Road, tel: (02) 3742 7654/3385 5016).

In the Sinai, Bedouins in Dahab and Nuwayba can provide camels for memorable rides through mountain and oases landscapes along the Gulf of Aqaba. A tip for hagglers: open negotiations with half the price asked. The Adrere Amellal Hotel in Siwah has some wonderful horses for experienced riders.

HIKING

Anyone planning to hike in Egypt needs to be fit: the climate is not ideal by any means. Hikers should also be aware that Sinai Bedouins are often appalled at the lack of respect for their sacred borders. You can walk in the St Catherine Protectorate provided you go with a Bedouin guide, tel: (069) 347 0457 Sheikh Musa.

Felucca rides

A great way to relax after a day of sightseeing is to rent a *felucca* in the late afternoon and watch the sunset. They cost between LE15–20 an hour, and can be taken in Cairo from opposite the Nile Hilton or near the Meridien Hotel, in Luxor and Aswan along the Corniche. It is still possible to sail a *felucca* between Luxor and Aswan in three or four days. Always agree on a price beforehand.

BALLOON TRIPS

Taking a balloon trip above the Valley of the Kings is a great but expensive experience: around US$250 per person including champagne breakfast. Trips can be booked in Luxor, **Hod Hod Sulayman**, tel: (095) 237 0116, **Balloons over Egypt**, tel: (095) 237 6515, **Magic Horizon**, tel: (065) 236 5060.

DESERT TOURS

Car trips out into the desert without four-wheel drive, careful planning and the right equipment are tantamount to suicide – one reason why unauthorised desert tours are forbidden. Soldiers can confiscate vehicles that travel away from the main roads and their drivers can expect several days in prison. Cars with four-wheel drive (they can be hired from the major rental car companies) are compulsory, as is at least one accompanying vehicle.

Valuable information about the desert and the oases can be found in *The Western Desert of Egypt: An Explorer's Handbook* by Cassandra Vivian, available from good bookshops in Egypt. There are some excellent desert guides too: Amr Shannon, tel: (02) 2519 6894, Khalifa Expedition, tel: (02) 847 3260; www.khalifaexp.com and Hisham Nessim, tel: (010) 188 1368. In Siwah one of the best guides is Abdallah Baghi, tel: (03) 460 1111; shali55@hotmail.com.

CAMEL MARKETS

Camels are driven 1,000 miles along the Darb al arba'ain ('forty-day way') from Sudan to Egypt, to markets in Cairo and Daraw (a 30-minute drive north of Aswan). The camel traders, farmers and butchers start haggling on Tuesdays from seven in the morning. Cairo's camel market is at Birqash, 45km (28 miles) north-west of the city centre (daily but most animated on Monday and Friday mornings).

PRACTICAL INFORMATION

Getting There

BY PLANE

Egypt Air, www.egyptair.com, and British Airways, www.britishairways.com, offer daily non-stop flights from London Heathrow to Cairo. Egypt Air also offers a weekly direct flight between Heathrow and Luxor. In addition to scheduled flights, it is worth investigating charter flights from Heathrow and Gatwick, especially to Luxor, Hurghadah, Aswan, Alexandria and Sharm al-Shaykh. Egypt Air in London, tel: (020) 7734 2395. British Airways in UK, tel: (0870) 850 9850.

Egypt Air also has up to five weekly flights between New York and Cairo; Egypt Air in New York, tel: (212) 581 5600; Mon–Fri 9am–5.30pm. Other major airlines also ply the route, but usually with a European stopover.

Anyone buying a single ticket rather than a package deal should certainly compare prices: they can vary a lot. One London travel company specialising in Egypt and offering good deals on major carriers is Soliman Travel, 113 Earls Court Road, SW5 9RL, tel: (020) 7244 6855.

Cairo International Airport has improved enormously in recent years.

FROM THE AIRPORT

All airports in Egypt have a taxi service and the fare to the nearest city/town centre is fixed. That said, it is sensible to check the current fare at the airport information desk or with a friendly travel representative before leaving the terminal: the taxi drivers that ply the airport route often try to hike up fares.

In Cairo, the Airport Bus Service operates from Terminal 1 to Maydan al-Tahrir (the main square near the Egyptian Museum), Mohandeseen and along the Pyramids Road. There is no fixed timetable: as soon as the bus is full, it sets off. Regular city buses also run to the airport; however, these are not recommended, as they are slow, uncomfortable and crowded.

OVERLAND FROM ISRAEL

The most direct way to travel from Egypt to Israel and the Palestinian Territories is via Rafah. But the border crossing here is frequently closed these days, so check with the Israeli embassy before leaving. And bear in mind that this route is not recommended as long as the troubles last. Most people travel instead via Taba in North-Eastern Sinai. A visa is not required for most nationalities to enter Israel, but for Egypt you will need a visa in advance, from the consulate in Eilat. If travelling by car, visitors are required to fulfil certain entry regulations: **1)** the car must have an International Carnet de Passage; **2)** the owner or a member of his/her family must be in the car; **3)** the driver should carry a valid international driver's licence; **4)** vehicle insurance must be taken out at the customs point; **5)** the car must run on gasoline (not diesel).

Getting Around

BY PLANE

Egypt Air, www.egyptair.com, has a good network of domestic flights, connecting Cairo, Alexandria, Luxor, Aswan, Abu Simbel, Hurghadah, Sharm al-Shaykh, the Monastery of St Catherine, Al-Arish (on the eastern Mediterranean), Mersa Matruh (western Mediterranean) and the New Valley in the Libyan Desert. There are several Air Sinai flights a week to the Egyptian-Israeli border town of Taba, and to other Sinai resorts.

BY TRAIN

The railway is a good option for travel between Cairo and Alexandria. The journey takes about two hours, and first-class carriages are comfortable with air-conditioning. Tickets can be bought at Ramesses Station (ideally on the day before departure). Train travel for foreigners is restricted to certain trains.

Cairo to Aswan via Luxor is another rail route popular with tourists (in view of the current terrorist threat, check that train rides through Upper Egypt are considered safe before booking). Trains with comfortable sleeper compartments leave Cairo around 7.45pm, arriving at Luxor and Aswan the following morning. Sleepers should be reserved a week in advance from Wagons Lits at Ramesses Station, tel: (02) 2574 9474; www.sleepingtrains.com or tel: (02) 2738 3682.

By carriage

Travelling by horse-drawn carriage *(calèche)* is a delightful way of seeing provincial cities and visiting outlying areas. In Luxor it is *de rigueur* to take a *calèche* along the Corniche to the Winter Palace Hotel for afternoon tea.

BY BUS

The most popular means of transport in Egypt is the bus. More and more companies connect far-flung regions of the country with its major cities. Tickets can be bought at the station or sometimes on the bus. On longer trips, it's best to call to check departure times, and to buy tickets a day in advance: check with the nearest tourist office in Cairo which terminus you need (there is a 24-hour information service at Cairo Airport).

Deluxe air-conditioned buses are comfortable, but avoid the 'Video Buses' unless you have earplugs. Cheaper buses are very crowded. In an attempt to keep inter-city buses out of the town centre traffic, many bus stations are relocated to the new Turgoman Garage, 600m (660 yards) southwest of Ramesses Station. At the time of writing there is still confusion as to where buses are leaving from, but the idea is that most will eventually leave from this one terminal. For now, check with each bus company. The main bus stations in Cairo are:

The West-Delta Bus Company, tel: (02) 2431 6742, operates buses to Alexandria, Marsa Matruh, Siwah and the Nile Delta.

The East Delta Bus Company, tel: (02) 2431 6723, runs buses to Sinai and the Canal Zone.

The Upper Egypt Bus Company, runs buses to everywhere south of Cairo including Fayyum, the Western desert oases and Red Sea Coast. Buses for Middle Egypt still leave from Aboud Bus Station on Sharia Shobra, 500m (550 yards) north of Ramesses Station. Buses for Luxor and Aswan, Western Desert oases and Red Sea Coast from Turgoman Garage.

Superjet runs more luxurious air conditioned buses to Egypt's main destinations.

BY TAXI

Taxis can be hailed by a wave in the street, and the destination then needs to be shouted at the driver. If he's carrying other passengers you can still get in, as long as your destination lies in the same direction. Meters never work, and locals just know what they should pay, but as a visitor it is safer to agree on a price before you start off.

Shared taxis, usually Peugeots, do cross-country trips on a regular basis. In Aswan, if you can't afford to take a plane to visit Abu Simbel, consider taking a station-wagon taxi – either shared with others (which is very cheap) or chartered (which allows more space for stretching out). These taxis do the journey in convoys.

RENTAL CARS

Cars can be hired at airports and big hotels from all the major international agencies, such as Avis, Budget and Hertz; jeeps with four-wheel drive are available. One-way rentals include a fee for recovering the vehicle. The cheapest offers start at around £15 a day. The cars offered by local companies are more likely to break down.

An international driving licence is needed, and no deposit is necessary if payment is made by credit card.

Rental cars in Cairo: Avis, tel: (02) 2579 2400, www.avisworld.com; Budget, tel: (02) 2265 2395, www.budget.com.

BY NILE STEAMER

The ancient sites on the Luxor–Aswan route can be comfortably viewed on four-day cruises. Prices vary according to the season, and are often negotiable, but it is usually cheaper to book a cruise abroad. The Cairo–Luxor route is considered a security risk at the moment, so check before leaving.

BICYCLES AND MOTORBIKES

Exhaust fumes and dangerous local drivers make cycling in Cairo a questionable pleasure, but a trip along the Nile in Luxor more than makes up for that: the larger hotels all provide bicycles for their guests, and there are also several hire outlets along the Corniche. Cyclists intending to visit the Valley of the Kings need to be in reasonably good condition, for the route is quite tough.

Motorbikes cannot be hired in Egypt. Bikers should bring their own machines with them for unforgettable tours of the Sinai, along the Red Sea coast and across the desert to the Nile Valley.

Facts for the Visitor

TRAVEL DOCUMENTS

Passports shown on arrival need to be valid for a minimum of six months. Visas are issued at the airport: buy a visa stamp at a bank counter and stick it into your passport, and the immigration official takes care of the rest. For just one trip to Egypt it's not worth organising a visa in your home country: they are more expensive.

Re-entry visas can also be obtained in Egypt itself: in Cairo, go to the Mugamma (Immigration Department), Maydan al-Tahrir, 1st floor (open daily 8am–1pm, closed Fri). The same office deals with visa extensions, for which a passport photograph is necessary.

The registration of passports is no longer necessary. Those leaving Egypt for other Arab countries should not carry an Israeli immigration stamp in their passports. It's a good idea to keep a photocopy of your passport somewhere safe.

CUSTOMS REGULATIONS

Items for personal use can be brought in and out of the country without being declared, but expensive equipment might be recorded in your passport.

TOURIST INFORMATION

Tourist information is available from the Egyptian State Tourist Office.
In the UK
Egyptian Tourist Office, 170 Piccadilly, London W1V 9DD, tel: (020) 7493 5283; brochure line: (0900) 160 0299.
In the US
630 Fifth Avenue, Suite 1706, New York, NY 1011, tel: (212) 332 2570; fax: (212) 956 6439; 8383 Wilshire Boulevard, Suite 215, Beverly Hills, Los Angeles, CA 90211, tel: (323) 653 8815; fax: (323) 653 8961; 645 North Michigan Avenue, Suite 829, Chicago, IL 60611, tel: (312) 280 4666; fax: (312) 280 4788.

In Egypt
Cairo: 5, Sh Adly, Downtown, tel: (02) 2391 3454. **Alexandria**: Maydan Saad Zaghlul, Ramleh Station, tel: (03) 484 3380. **Luxor**: On the Corniche in the 'Tourist Bazaar', tel: (095) 237 2215. **Aswan**: Tourist Information at the station and at Midan al-Mahatta, tel: (097) 231 2811. **Hurghadah**: Tourist Information opposite Grand Hotel in New Hurghadah, tel: (065) 344 4420.

CURRENCY AND EXCHANGE

The exchange rate of the Egyptian pound (Livre Egyptienne, or LE) is linked to that of the US dollar, so black market exchange has no attractions. One Egyptian pound is subdivided into 100 piastres (PT). There are 200, 100, 50, 20, 10, 5 and 1 pound banknotes in circulation (and notes for 50, 25 and 10 piastres). Coins are 1LE, 25PT and 10PT.

Credit cards (American Express, Visa, Euro/MasterCard and Diner's Club) are accepted by all international hotels, as well as many shops and restaurants – who often add a bank commission of 3–5 percent. Many banks can provide cash advances on Euro/MasterCard and Visa.

EXCHANGE REGULATIONS

You are allowed to import up to LE1,000. However, as the exchange rate offered by banks outside Egypt is very poor, you are advised to change money/traveller's cheques on arrival. Banks at airports provide 24-hour exchange facilities. Always count your money, and compare the amount with the sum mentioned on the receipt.

Egyptian currency can be converted back into US dollars on leaving the country if exchange receipts are shown. Customs declarations should be filled out at the airport for any larger amounts of currency being taken in or out of the country.

TIPPING

Baksheesh is generally around 5 percent of the full sum – slightly less if a bill is very high, and slightly more if it is lower. Chambermaids should be given around LE30 per week, porters LE5–10 and lift boys and doormen LE5. Staff after *baksheesh* will offer you all manner of – often unwished-for – assistance.

There's no obligation to pay, but do remember the gravity of the unemployment situation (and that giving alms is considered a duty in Islam). So have change ready. Taxi drivers can be particularly tough, however, and any complaints they make should be studiously ignored; their fares usually contain an illegal 'foreigner surcharge'.

OPENING TIMES

Shops
Shop opening and closing times vary a great deal, though common hours are 9am–1pm and 4.30–8pm. Most close on Friday.
Banks
Saturday–Thursday, 8.30am–2pm, but many of the larger hotels often have a 24-hour service.
Post offices
Usually open Saturday to Thursday, 8am–3pm.
Government offices
8am–2pm daily except Friday.

POST OFFICES

Letters and cards can often take a long time to reach Europe and North America from Egypt. Courier services such as the Express Mail Service (EMS) are far more reliable, and a standard letter will usually reach Europe within around three days. Important or urgent documents are best entrusted to the door-to-door courier service DHL in Cairo, tel: (02) 3302 9801, fax: (02) 3302 9810.

TIME

Egypt is two hours ahead of Greenwich Mean Time and seven hours ahead of Eastern Seaboard Time.

VOLTAGE

Despite the fact that Egypt runs on 220v, it's best to bring some adapters with you because plugs seem to come in all shapes and sizes. Power cuts (often lasting for hours) are common. Batteries are cheap, but short-lived.

WEIGHTS AND MEASURES

Egypt has now adopted the metric system, and all weights are in kilos and distances are in kilometres.

CLOTHING

Summer clothing is usually fine the whole year round. During the winter months in Cairo and north of it, a warm pullover and an umbrella are useful; a pullover or fleece is also a good idea for the cool nights in Upper (ie. southern) Egypt and on the Red Sea. Bring sturdy footwear for visits to the Pyramids, the Valley of the Kings and other temple areas. Women should dress unprovocatively. Underdressed men, meanwhile, including male tourists dressed in shorts or without shirts, can be treated as objects of scorn. Walking barefoot is a sign of absolute poverty and is much frowned upon too.

TOPLESS BATHING

This is utterly forbidden everywhere, even on beaches and around hotel swimming pools, but it still occurs illegally at some Red Sea resorts.

WOMEN TRAVELLING ALONE

Women travelling in Egypt on their own are considered exotic, and men will often make advances. Tight jeans, miniskirts and skimpy tops are all considered sexually provocative in Egypt. Women are advised to wear baggy, modest clothing and walk in a determined manner. If this doesn't deter advances, you may try to 'expose' the culprit by shouting loudly at him. Friendly pats on the shoulder and eye contact, harmless in Western Europe, are often misinterpreted as sexual invitations. Stories about one's husband and children – whether real or invented – make many would-be suitors back off. Invitations to men's apartments should be declined politely but firmly by women travelling alone.

PHOTOGRAPHY

Everything can be photographed – apart from airports, stations, harbours, military installations, the Suez Canal and also the restricted areas around harbours at Port Said and Suez.

When photographing people be sure to put on a friendly smile and ask permission politely; a small tip will also be much appreciated. Women usually don't like to be photographed.

Photography is allowed in most museums, temples and tombs, but for a fee: LE10–20 for using a camera, up to LE100 for a tripod, and LE150–200 for a video camera. Ordinary film (but not slide film and memory cards) can be obtained in most places. Bring batteries and chargers for digital cameras.

> **Public holidays**
> The following are the official public holidays of the Gregorian calendar: 1 January (New Year), 22 February (Day of Unity), 25 April (Liberation of Sinai), 1 May (Labour Day), 18 June (Anniversary of British troop withdrawal), 23 July (Anniversary of 1952 Revolution), 23 September (Victory over Israel 1956), 6 October (Day of the Armed Forces), 24 October (Entry into Suez 1973), 23 December (Victory Day).
> For religious holidays see page 107.

NEWSPAPERS

The Egyptian Gazette, founded in 1880, is a daily English-language newspaper. It has a Saturday edition called *The Egyptian Mail*. The only articles of real interest in either of these publications are those on culture, tourism and archaeology, since both follow a strict pro-government line.

The weekly English-language paper *Al-Ahram Weekly* is a particularly good read. Informative articles on culture, music, theatre, literature and events in general can be found in the monthly magazine *Egypt Today*, www.egypttoday.com. It also has useful restaurant guide.

RADIO

The BBC World Service broadcasts on FM95 from 6.45am–10.15am, 1–2pm, 3–9pm: and on 1325 KHz from 5pm–1.15am. News is on the hour. The Voice of America broadcasts on several wavelengths.

In addition to these there is European Radio Cairo, which broadcasts in a variety of European languages.

TELEPHONE AND FAX

Local calls can be made from phone booths and at post offices (long queues). Egypt has similar cheap rates to Europe. A three-minute minimum fee is still charged by private telephone offices, and by hotels too (sometimes even when the phone doesn't get picked up after five rings).

Bring your own mobile phone as Vodafone and Mobinil can connect to your network. Consider buying an Egyptian SIM card for a local number and cheaper rates.

Faxes are best sent from private telephone offices, which can be found all over the place.

International dialling codes: Egypt 0020; UK 0044; USA 001 (each followed by the area code minus the initial zero).

Codes within Egypt: Cairo 02, Alexandria and Marsa Matruh 03, Luxor 095, Aswan and Abu Simbel 097, Hurghadah 065, Sinai and Suez 062, Port Said 064, Bur Safagah 065, Fayyum 084, Al-Isma'iliyyah 064, Tanta 040.

AT&T: 2356 0200; MCI: 2355 5770; if calling from outside Cairo dial 02 before both numbers.

EGYPT ON THE INTERNET

There are hundreds of websites on Egypt. Here are some of the more general ones:

www.sis.gov.eg: Egypt's State Information Service, including tourism.

www.egypttoday.com: general interest magazine of cultural and current events.

www.egypt.travel: official site of the Ministry of Tourism.

www.travellersinegypt.org: historical travel accounts.

www.yallabina.com: Everything you need to know about nightlife and what's on in Cairo.

Internet cafés are sprouting up all over Egypt, and hotels often offer computers for the use of their guests.

BOOKSHOPS

Lehnert and Landrock, 44 Sharia Sherif, Downtown, has a good selection of books as well as old photographs and postcards of Egypt. Another of their shops, tel: (02) 2575 8006, is opposite the entrance of the Egyptian Museum. In Zamalek there is **Diwan**, 159 Sharia 26th-of-July, with a great selection of books, Arabic videos/DVDs and music, as well as a good café where you can browse over a coffee. **L'Orientale**, Shop 757 in the basement of the Nile Hilton Shopping Mall, Midan al-Tahrir, Downtown, has antiquarian Oriental books, maps and prints.

Health

To prevent diarrhoea, avoid the following: unpeeled fruit, raw vegetables, salads, ice cream, ice-cubes in drinks, fruit juices and unboiled water. Prevent dehydration of the body tissues by drinking a lot (but no alcoholic or iced drinks), and add more salt than usual to your food too. A midday rest is also helpful.

Don't swim in the Nile – it's very badly polluted. Don't put as much as a finger into any of its tributaries, or into any stagnant water anywhere: parasites can penetrate the body and cause bilharzia.

Carrying your own medical kit is a good idea when travelling off the beaten track. The basic equipment should include: sun-cream with a high protection factor; medicine against fever, colds, pain, insect bites and digestive and circulatory complaints; bandages and plasters; and also disinfectant and water purification tablets if necessary. Those planning desert trips should make sure they take along snakebite kits.

VACCINATIONS

Vaccinations are not compulsory, but polio and tetanus jabs are both recommended, as are malaria tablets and hepatitis injections if you intend to make desert and oasis trips.

HEALTH INSURANCE

Foreigners must pay for all medical care in advance of treatment. It is therefore essential to take out suitable health insurance before travelling so that you can claim back any expenses incurred. If you plan to dive or take part in water sports, make sure you are covered adequately. Repatriation insurance in case of serious accident is also a good idea.

MEDICAL ASSISTANCE

Medical standards outside the capital are not usually up to Western European standards. Egyptian doctors are trained to deal with minor ailments (hotels can help); more serious cases should be referred to hospitals. Emergencies should be treated at the Al-Salaam International Hospital in Cairo-Maadi, Corniche al-Nil, tel: (02) 2524 0250; emergencies: (02) 2524 0077, or the Anglo-American Hospital, Zohoreja, near Cairo Tower, tel: (02) 2735 6162. A considerable sum needs to be paid in advance for any stay in hospital.

Chemists can be found everywhere; medicine is usually available without prescription and is a lot cheaper than in Western Europe.

EMERGENCIES

Police, tel: 122
Ambulance, tel: 123
Fire brigade, tel: 180
Tourist police, tel: 126

CRIME

Generally speaking, Egypt is quite a safe place, and Egyptians are honest people. Robberies and muggings are rare, but pickpockets and conmen are not uncommon in the more popular tourist areas.

The British Foreign Office issues advice to travellers: tel: (020) 7238 4503/4 or log onto www.fco.gov.uk/travel Caution is advised if you plan to travel through the provinces of Asyut, Qena, Al-Minya and Sohag. The trip from Cairo to Luxor is better done by plane.

If you intend to journey between the Red Sea and Qena *(see page 89)*, you are strongly advised to do so in an armed convoy. *See also the box on travel restrictions on page 53.*

DIPLOMATIC REPRESENTATION

UK: 7 Sharia Ahmed Ragheb, Garden City, Cairo, tel: (02) 2794 0850/2/8.
US: 5 Sharia Latin America, Garden City, Cairo, tel: (02) 2797 3300.

ACCOMMODATION

HOTELS

Hotels registered with the Egyptian Hotel Association are allocated one-to five-stars. This is often one or two stars too high when compared to Western equivalents. People planning to go to Egypt during peak holiday time are strongly advised to book in advance.

Last-minute bookings are recommended for anyone planning to travel to Egypt out of season. Always enquire about special offers, package deals and price reductions.

A 19 percent hotel tax is levied by the government: check to make sure it's included in the price; in upmarket establishments it usually is not.

The hotel selection below is listed according to the following categories:
€€€€ = very expensive
€€€ = expensive
€€ = moderate
€ = inexpensive.

Alexandria

Green Plaza Hilton Alexandria, 14th of May Bridge, Smouha, tel: (03) 420 9120; www.hilton.com. Twenty minute-ride away from the centre, but the most luxurious rooms in town with all mod-cons. €€€–€€€€
Hotel Union, 164 Sharia 26th of July, tel: (03) 480 7312. Excellent budget option with very clean en-suite rooms and some with a balcony. €
Paradise Inn Metropole, 52 Zaghlul St (Ramleh Station), tel: (03) 486 1465; www.paradiseinnegypt.com. Classy old hotel, recently renovated, overlooking Maydan Zaghlul. €€–€€€
Sofitel Cecil, Maydan Zaghlul, Ramleh Station, tel: (03) 483 7173, fax: (03) 485 5655. This hotel with a lot of history offers pleasant rooms overlooking the Eastern Harbour. The service can be extremely slow. €€€

Aswan

Keylany Hotel, 25 Sharia Keylani, off main Sharia as-Suq, tel: (097) 231 7332; www.keylanyhotel.com. Friendly and central budget hotel with spotless rooms. €
Old Cataract Sofitel Sh Abdal et-Tahrir, tel: (097) 231 6000; www.sofitel.com. This colonial-style building, overlooking the Nile and Elephantine Island, is undoubtedly one of Egypt's most romantic hotels. €€€€
Orchid St George, Shari' Muhamed Khalid, tel: (097) 231 5997; email: orchidahotel@hotmail.com. Small, clean, modern hotel; check the room before you take it. €€
Sarah Hotel, on a cliff, just south of Nubian Museum, tel: (097) 232 7234; www.sarahotel-aswan.com. Quiet hotel with great views over the Nile and the desert on the other side with spacious rooms, some with big balconies. €€

Cairo

Cairo Marriott, 16 Sh Saray al-Gezira, Zamalek, tel: (02) 2728 3000, fax: (02) 2728 3001; www.marriott.com. Formerly Ismail Pasha's Gezira Palace, the Marriott offers outstanding restaurants and service. €€€€
Carlton, 21 Sharia 26th of July, Downtown, tel: (02) 2575 2323; email: carlton@menanet.net. Charming downtown budget hotel in 1950s style with a pleasant rooftop café. €
Cosmopolitan, off Sh Qasr en-Nil, Downtown, tel: (02) 2393 6914, fax: (02) 3393 3531. Comfortable rooms in a grand Art Nouveau building, located in a quiet alley in the city centre. €€
Four Seasons Cairo, First Residence, 35 Sh Giza, Giza, tel: (02) 3573 1212; www.fourseasons.com. Most luxurious hotel in town, with views over the Nile and Pyramids on the horizon. €€€€

Golden Tulip Flamenco Hotel, 2 Gezirat el-Wusta, Zamalik, tel: (02) 2735 0815; www.flamencohotels.com. Comfortable, peaceful hotel in residential Zamalik, near many restaurants, and overlooking the Nile. €€

Mena House Oberoi, Sharia al-Haram, at the foot of the Giza Pyramid, Giza, tel: (02) 3383 3222; www. oberoihotels.com. Old-style palace rooms where you wake up with the Pyramids on your doorstep. €€€€

Nile Hilton, Midan Tahrir, Downtown, tel: (02) 2578 0444; www.hilton.com. Cairo's first five-star hotel, opposite the Egyptian Museum and facing the Nile. €€€

Osiris, 49 Sh Nubar, Downtown, tel: (02) 2794 5728, fax: (02) 2794 2981; www.osiris.fr.fm. Small, very central family-run hotel, with 15 rooms. €

Windsor, 19 Sharia Alfi Bey, Downtown, tel: (02) 2591 5277; www.windsor cairo.com. Colonial-style hotel with lots of run-down charm. Rooms vary from huge to cramped, some with ancient bathrooms. Great bar. €€

Dahab

Coral Coast, Asilah, tel: (069) 364 1195, fax: (069) 364 1691; www.embah. com. Locally run place along beachfront, with 29 rooms and own dive centre. €€

Hilton Dahab Resort, tel: (069) 364 0310; www.hilton.com. White-domed rooms and two great swimming pools. €€€€

Nesima Resort, on the beach in Mashraba, tel: (069) 364 0320; www. nesima-resort.com. Beautiful hotel, with domed rooms and a great pool. €€€

Al-Gouna

Captain's Inn, Abu Tig Marina, tel/fax: (065) 358 0170; email: captainsinn@ elgouna.com. Boutique guest house overlooking the marina and close to the nightlife at Abu Tig Marina. €€

Sheraton Miramar, Al-Gouna bay, tel: (065) 354 5606. A Disneyesque fantasy by architect Michael Graves. €€€€

Hurghadah

Sahl Hasheesh Oberoi, On the Sahl Hasheesh coast, 25 minutes south of Hurghada, tel: (065) 344 0777; www. oberoihotel.com. The most exclusive all-suite luxury hotel on this coast. €€€€

Sea View, Corniche Street, Ed-Dahar, tel: (065) 354 5959, fax: (065) 354 6779; www.seaviewhotel.com.eg. Family-run hotel in a prime seafront location. Excellent value and high standards. €

Shedwan Garden, Corniche Road, Ed-Dahar, tel: (065) 355 5052, fax: (065) 355 5054; www.redseahotels.com. Large, older-style complex with a vast expanse of beach and a holiday-camp kind of atmosphere. €€–€€€

Zak Royal Wings, Sheraton Road, Sigala, tel: (065) 344 6012; www.zak hotel.com. This older-style hotel is ideal for families. In a great location near the beach, shops and many family restaurants, and all 41 rooms have a balcony overlooking the large pool. €€

Luxor

Al-Moudira, 5km (3 miles) from the main sights on the West bank, tel: (012) 325 1307; www.moudira.com. Modern, luxury hotel. €€€€

Amun al-Gezira, Gezirat al-Bayrat, West Bank, tel: (095) 231 0912. Modern, family-run hotel surrounded by a lush garden and fields. Great views from the rooftop terrace. €

Nur el Qurna, opposite Gurna ticket office, West Bank, tel: (095) 231 1430. Beautiful budget hotel set in a garden, with simple but stylish rooms overlooking the sugarcane fields. €–€€

Philippe, Sh Dr Labib Habashy, tel: (095) 237 2284; www.philippeluxorhotel.com. Great value in the heart of the city. Book well ahead. €€

Sofitel Winter Palace, Corniche al-Nil, tel: (095) 238 0425; www.sofitel.com. Colonial-style hotel with beautiful architecture, a large garden and big comfortable rooms, but not very good service. €€€€

Monastery of St Catherine

Daniela, St Catherine's Village, tel: (069) 347 0379; www.daniela-hotels.com. Stone-built hotel in a spectacular location, with 74 small chalets and villas. An ideal place to stay for a morning visit to the monastery or an attempt to climb Mount Sinai. €€
Monastery Hostel, Monastery of St Catherine, tel/fax: (069) 347 0353; email: moussaboules@yahoo.com. Monastic, spartan rooms but clean with aircon. Stunning location, as close to Mount Moses as you can get. Half board only. €€

Nuwayba

Habiba, Nuwayba City, tel: (069) 350 0770; www.sinai4you.com/habiba. Clean airconditioned bungalows and a good restaurant. €–€€
Hilton Coral Hotel, tel: (069) 352 0320; www.hilton.com. Luxurious holiday resort with nice pools. €€€

Al-Qusayr

Mangrove Bay, south of al-Qusayr, tel: (065) 325 2821; email: mangrove@egypt-online.com. Tranquil hotel on a wonderful sandy beach with some of the best diving/snorkelling. €€–€€€
Møvenpick Sirena Beach, Al-Quadim Bay, tel: (065) 333 2100, fax: (065) 333 2128; www.movenpick-hotels.com. Delightful resort hotel on one of the best snorkelling beaches on the Red Sea, with domed bungalows and several pools. €€€–€€€€

Bur Safagah

Nemo Dive Club/Hotel, Maglis Madina, Corniche Street, tel: (065) 325 6777; www.nemodive.com. Great-value all-inclusive Belgian/Dutch-managed hotel 3km (2 miles) north of the main cen-

tre. 30 rooms. Wonderful views from the rooftop restaurant and bar. €€

Sharm al-Shaykh

Eden Rock, Na'ama Bay Heights, tel: (069) 360 2250; fax: (069) 360 2257; www.edenrockhotel.net. Quieter hotel recently refurbished in an old Viennese boutique style. Wonderful views across Na'ama Bay from the terraced pool. €€€
Marriott Beach Resort, Na'ama Bay, tel: (069) 360 0190; fax: (069) 360 0188; www.marriott.com. Large resort with over 500 rooms in a great location. The indoor pools even have waterfalls. The Marriott 'mountain' resort is set further back across Peace Road. €€€€
Ritz-Carlton, Ras Umm Sid, tel: (069) 366 1919; fax: (069) 366 1920; www.ritzcarlton.com. All 321 guest rooms have a private terrace and the latest facilities. Several top quality restaurants and a cigar lounge. €€€€
Umbi Diving Village, Shark's Bay, tel: (069) 360 0942; fax: (069) 360 0944; www.sharksbay.com. One of the original resorts, with a relaxing atmosphere. Choice of beach cabins, bamboo huts or rooms in the Bedouin Village perched on a small clifftop. Private beach with a beautiful coral reef and an excellent fish restaurant. €€

Siwah

Adrere Amellal, on Siwah Lake, 20km (12 miles) from Siwah Town, tel: (02) 2736 7879; www.adrereamellal.net. Stunning eco-lodge built using mud and salt crystals. The pool under the palm trees is an extension of the natural spring that feeds the oasis. Food straight from the organic garden. No phones or electricity. €€€€
Shali Lodge, Maydan as Souk, Sh al Seboukha, Siwah town, tel: (046) 460 1299, fax: (046) 460 1799. Eight big, comfortable rooms set around a small pool. Rooms are decorated in local style, and the food is delightful. €€

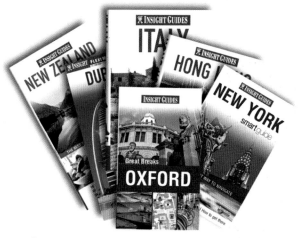

INDEX